FAITH UNDER FIRE

Lieutenant Colonel Canon F.G. Scott wearing an anti-gas respirator.
Canadian War Museum.

Faith Under Fire

Frederick G. Scott

Canada's Extraordinary Chaplain of the Great War

ALAN HUSTAK

Véhicule Press

Published with the generous assistance of the Canada Council for the Arts, the Canada Book Fund of the Department of Canadian Heritage, and the Société de développement des entreprises culturelles du Québec (SODEC).

Cover design: David Drummond
Map by Yannick Allen Larochelle.
Typeset in Minion and Mrs Eaves by Simon Garamond
Printed by Marquis Printing Inc.

LIBRARY AND ARCHIVES CANADA CATALOGUING IN PUBLICATION

Hustak, Alan, 1944-, author
Faith under fire : Frederick G. Scott, Canada's extraordinary
chaplain
of the Great War / Alan Hustak.

Includes excerpts from unpublished letters of Frederick G. Scott
held at the McCord Museum.

ISBN 978-1-55065-375-5 (pbk.)

1. Scott, Frederick George, 1861-1944. 2. World War, 1914-1918–
Chaplains–Canada–Biography. 3. Canada. Canadian Army. Canadian
Infantry Division, 1st–Chaplains–Biography. 4. Military chaplains–
Canada–Biography. 5. Priests–Québec (Province)–Québec–Biography.
6. St. Matthew's Anglican Church (Québec, Québec)–Clergy–Biography.
7. Poets, Canadian (English)–Québec (Province)–Québec–Biography.
8. Québec (Québec)–Biography. I. Title. II. Title: Frederick G. Scott,
Canada's extraordinary chaplain of the Great War.

D639.C38H88 2014   940.4'78092   C2014-900597-0

Published by Véhicule Press, Montréal, Québec, Canada
www.vehiculepress.com

Distribution in Canada by LitDistCo
www.litdistco.ca

Distributed in the U.S. by Independent Publishers Group
www.ipgbook.com

Printed in Canada on FSC certified paper

For Michael Rudder, who not only portrayed him,
but like Scott, knew what it was to be wounded.

CONTENTS

Canon Frederick Scott's
"parish" during the Great War

North Sea

London

ENGLAND

English Channel

Dunkirk
Calais
Boulogne-sur-Mer
Étaples

FLANDERS
Ypres
Messines
Neuve-Chapelle
Langemarck
Passchendaele
Loos
Vimy
Arras
Cambrai
Bapaume
Albert
Péronne
Amiens

Brussels

BELGIUM

Mons
Charleroi

Somme

FRANCE

Oise
Soissons
Château-Thierry
Marne
Reims

Seine

Paris

Preface

I FIRST HEARD OF CANON FREDERICK SCOTT in 2006 on a military firing range at St-Bruno, Quebec where I had gone to interview Justin Trudeau, who was making his movie acting debut on the set of *The Great War,* Brian McKenna's docudrama about the Battle of Passchendaele. An actor friend of mine, Michael Rudder, was portraying Scott in the film. When Rudder told me about his character and mentioned the creative differences he was having with his director over his interpretation of the role, the antics of an aging Anglican chaplain on a World War I battlefield didn't really resonate with me. I was much more interested in the character that Trudeau was playing, Major Talbot Papineau, a historical figure that I was not only much more familiar with but admired. Had Papineau not been killed he might have been prime minister of Canada instead of Mackenzie King.

It wasn't until five years later when I was commissioned to write a centennial history of the Royal Montreal Regiment that I discovered more about this poet/priest who dug the remains of his dead son out of the mud following the Battle of the Somme. How, I wondered, could a priest exposed to that kind of horror, continue to believe in and serve his God? After learning the bare bones of Scott's life and reading his book, *The Great War as I Saw It,* Nora Hague at Montreal's McCord Museum directed me to his personal papers. They reveal someone whose most endearing traits were a self-deprecating sense of humour and his deep Catholic faith. His whole being comes through his letters, as one writer put it, as someone "buoyant with pleasure."

I would be remiss if I did not thank the many others who encouraged the project and helped me write this account. I am indebted to Lieutentant Colonel Colin Robinson who commissioned me to write the history of the Royal Montreal Regiment, and who shares with me his admiration for Canon Scott.

I am especially indebted to Scott's great-great grandsons, Quebec MNA Geoff Kelley and his brother Stephen Kelley (their youngest brother, incidentally, is veteran CBC journalist, Mark Kelley); Canada's language commissioner, Graham Fraser, whose parents shared a cottage in North Hatley with F.R. Scott's family; and to archivist and publisher Nancy Marrelli who was pressed into service as a research assistant.

In Ottawa, I am grateful to Lara Andrews at the Military History Research Centre and to Susan Ross at the National War Museum for their help. Elizabeth Gibson and Eamon Duffy at the McGill University library, Barbara McPherson archivist at the Anglican Diocese of Montreal, Charles Taker, Céline Widmer, Julian Putkowski in England, co-author of *Murderous Tommies*, who generously responded patiently and quickly by e-mail to my queries. I drew on a number of other books, including Sandra Djwa's biography, *The Politics of the Imagination: A Life of F.R. Scott*; Major Francis Bethel Ware's unpublished manuscript, *Canon Scott as I knew Him*, Tim Cook's majestic two-volume history of the First World War, *At the Sharp End: Canadians Fighting the Great War, 1914-1916*, and *Shock Troops: Canadians Fighting the Great War, 1917-1918*; Adam Hochschild's *To End All Wars: A Story of Loyalty and Rebellion, 1914-1918*; Duff Crearer's *Padres in No Man's Land: Canadian Chaplains and the Great War*; and Peter Hanson's *Muddling Through: The Organisation of the British Army Chaplaincy in World War One*.

Special thanks to graphic artist Yannick Allen Larochelle.

I am fortunate in having wonderful publishers—Simon Dardick and Nancy Marrelli—to whom I owe a great deal.

Montreal – Fort Qu'Appelle 2014

A.M.D.G.

F. G. Scott's father, Dr. William Edward Scott, taught anatomy at McGill. *Courtesy of Stephen S. Kelley.*

Chapter One

FREDERICK GEORGE SCOTT was born in Montreal April 7, 1861, in the 24th year of Queen Victoria's long reign and died January 19, 1944. His parents were evangelical Anglicans; his father, Dr. William Edward Scott was an Englishman who came to Canada in 1831 to teach anatomy at McGill University and also worked as a medical officer with the Grand Trunk Pacific Railway. His mother, Elizabeth Sproston, was a sickly but determined woman who lost five of her nine children to tuberculosis before Frederick was born.

He grew up on Union Avenue where, because of his mother's chronic illness, he was raised by a nanny, Matilda Preddy. Scott was six years old at the time of Confederation. One of his earliest recollections was hearing the cannons on the McGill campus fire the twenty-one gun salute to the new nation on July 1, 1867. He was ten years old when he wrote his first poem for his Aunt Tilly:

> There is dew for the floweret,
> and honey for the bee,
> and bowers for the wild bird,
> and love for you and me.

The poems he wrote later in his life, while sometimes maudlin and infused with an air of mourning and melancholy, sprang from genuine feeling, and record emotion to which everyone can easily relate. He attended high school in Montreal, but it was as a boy vacationing in the Laurentian wilderness where Scott first encountered what he described as "the awesome silence of God." His ministry began with a specific call; God, he believed, does call people. Throughout his lifetime he would often quote from the 19th Psalm, "The heavens declare the Glory of God, and the firmament showeth his handy work."

As a product of his times, Scott also had unwavering faith in the sanctity of the British Empire and its Imperial vision. When he came of age in the 1870s the Empire represented what was thought to be the best of western civilization. It was a time in which the crosses on the Union Jack were regarded with absolute certainty as symbols not only of a British, but a world-wide Christian empire in which military conquest in the Queen's name was equal to spiritual conquest in Christ's name.

His idealism was constricted by his parents' austere evangelical Church of England religiosity. He was also confused by the discussions on Darwin, creationism and evolution. His parents were evangelicals, and warned their son to stay away from St. John the Evangelist, a new Anglo-Catholic church which had just opened in the city at the corner of President Kennedy and St-Urbain.. Not one to listen to authority, not even then, Scott went anyway and was impressed with its founding priest, Edmund Wood. He confessed to Wood that he thought he was losing his faith. "I am delighted to hear it, it means you are beginning to think," Wood replied. "Now I can do something with you."

Wood introduced the impressionable teenager to the Tractarian reform movement, and instilled in Scott the sacramental doctrines which would influence his entire spiritual life. Tractarians believed that Henry VIII had stripped the church of the mystery of faith and were bent on returning the Church of England to the supremacy of scripture, communion, confession and fasting, which had largely

I wish to express my present feelings
in poetry.

1st There is dew for the floweret,
And honey, for th bee.
And bowers for the wild bird,
And love for you & me.

2nd There are tears for the many,
And pleasures for the few;
But let the world pass on dear,
There's love for me & you.

All our pets are getting on well
except the silkworms for I have
only eight left, out of about a hundred &c.
We all went to church this morning
even Charley.

Scott's first poem appeared in a letter to his Aunt Tilly, June 18, 1871.
McCord Museum.

fallen by the wayside since the monarch became temporal head of the Church in the 16th century.

Leaders of this so-called Oxford movement—John Keble, Edward Pusey, Richard Froude and John Henry Newman—set out to divorce the Church from political influence and return it to the liturgical practices of the Anglo-Catholic church of medieval times—coloured vestments, incense and candles on the altar. In his tracts, Newman argued that there was nothing in doctrine to distinguish the Anglican church from the Roman Catholic church. He believed in the doctrine of transubstantiation, and in such practices as praying for the dead and private confession, which evangelicals denounced as "popery." Newman converted to Roman Catholicism. In 1879, without ever having been a member of the Roman Curia, he was named a cardinal by Pope Leo XIII. All of this bordered on heresy to the established Church of England, especially in Montreal, where anti-papal sentiment was widespread among the Protestant population.

Scott failed his freshman year at McGill and his educational progress continued at Bishop's University, where he obtained his arts Degree in 1881. In 1882 a teenaged sweetheart he intended to marry died. Heartbroken, Scott became a brooding romantic figure. His first attempt to have his introspective poetry published when he was nineteen was rejected; he was advised never to write again because his verse was "too gloomy." He enrolled in the theological college but Montreal's Bishop William Bond objected to Scott's high church practices. So in January 1883 Scott sailed to England to continue his religious studies at King's College.

"All the altars in the churches I have seen have candles and a crucifix on them, and would create a storm of abuse in Canada," he wrote to his mother shortly after his arrival. "Westminster Abbey is exquisite, but it is no use attempting to describe it. It entirely defies description, all around us were the tombs of the great men, but the hideous monuments consisting of dropsicle cherubs, bloated females and men in laurels and dressing gowns, put up I suppose in the tasteless 18th century, are quite out of harmony with the delicate beauty of the Abbey." A visit to Christopher Wren's masterpiece, St. Paul's Cathedral, left him cold. "It is a great big ungainly sort of building, that is for a church. I dare say, it would have made a good post office. It, like Westminster is also full of hideous monuments."

He arrived in England with about $40,000 in today's money. After paying $15,000 for his tuition and lodging, he went to London's Bond Street where he bought a handsome new wardrobe, an afternoon suit, "of the best material," a dress coat, "with a very rich silk collar," dress shirts, shoes "lined with crimson satin,-" calfskin gloves and a top hat. "I have heard that it is so important for a fellow to be well dressed when calling," he informed his mother, adding that while abroad he intended to make the best of all of his opportunities, "both in the college and without. " It seems he did. "I intend to attend one entertainment a week," he wrote home after seeing Sir Henry Irving and Ellen Terry in *Much Ado About Nothing* ("One of the finest pieces ever put on the stage, the scenery was magnificent, especially the church scene...").

In April he went to Birmingham to visit Cardinal Newman, the charismatic convert to Roman Catholicism who had led the Oxford movement.

Instead of the vigorous clergyman that Scott had imagined, he was introduced to a frail old man. "I will not say I was disappointed," Scott wrote of the meeting,

But I experienced a shock, the shock that everyone feels on first meeting a great man, one whom we have dreamt about, and one's imagination has clothed with ideal glory—face to face. The aged man before me who rose and gave me his hand, motioned me to a chair and tottered so feebly, I could hardly imagine it was the Newan of my dreams—the exquisite writer, the subtle reasoner, the form which was once tall and commanding was now bent nearly double with age and the face was shrunken and deeply furrowed with time. But on the face was a tender settled calm—the calm of evening—of the light which lingers in the sky after the light has gone behind the hills. And his eyes—such eyes. I shall never forget them; they had that dreamy, far off look in them which told of a pure soul within. To me there was something infinitely sad in the solitariness of the poor old man. No woman's hand was near to tend and comfort him; no children were there to bring back to the old memories of youth in which the aged find such solace. The generation in which he had really lived and moved had all gone, and he was left alone...but the very loneliness and isolation were a glory and a light separating him from ordinary men and casting around him the medieval colours of sainthood.

While studying for the priesthood, Scott's work with the destitute and his social concerns were so apparent that his mother cautioned him not to "go so much among the poor, miserable wretched people of London. I like you taking the little, miserable hungry children into bake shops and feeding them with buns, but take care my darling, you may be waylaid and robbed."

During Scott's first term that year, he learned that "something was wrong with his father's heart." He was prepared to return home but his father discouraged the idea, telling him "he was very anxious that nothing interfere with his college work." Dr. Scott died on May 24, 1883. He was sixty. Six months later on November 21, Scott's

F.G. Scott as a young man, taken in 1885.
Courtesy of Stephen S. Kelley.

mother, Elizabeth, died. Then his aunt died in January of 1884. Grief stricken, he came back to Canada where he spent several months at St. James the Apostle working with Father Edmund Wood. He was stirred by the news in the spring of 1885 of the massacre at Duck Lake, Saskatchewan—a skirmish in which twelve North West Mounted Police officers were killed in an ambush that sparked the Riel Uprising in Western Canada. He followed the news of the Rebellion with great interest. When the hostilities ended with the capture of Louis Riel at Batoche and Riel's subsequent hanging, Scott applauded John A. Macdonald's method of nation building, and was moved to write "In Memoriam" which commends the military "for the glory they have brought us," in the "Canadian North-West."

> Wild the prairie's grasses wave
> O'er each hero's new-made grave;
> . . .
> Where the call of duty led,
> Where the lonely prairies spread,
>
> Where for us they fought and bled,
> Our loved, our lost, our glorious dead!

Scott had hoped to be ordained in Montreal but Bishop Bond summarily dismissed Scott's Tractarian theology as "crude and contradictory," and refused Scott's application to become a priest. So Scott returned to England in 1886, where he was ordained by Bishop Thomas Leigh Claughton, a former professor of poetry at Oxford. The ceremony took place in St. Alban's Abbey, the oldest site of continuous Christian worship in Britain. In one letter home Scott remarked that his years in England had made him a better Catholic, and that he was glad that Bishop Bond had refused to ordain him.

He was offered a post in Coggeshall, Essex, and might have joined a cloistered order and remained in England except for the fact that he had become engaged to Amy Brooks, a crisp, practical woman from Chipping Barnet, which was then in Hertfordshire, just north of London. He had met her in Montreal where she had come in 1878 after her father died. Amy was originally cool to Scott's romantic overtures, but during a trip to see him in England in 1886 she confessed that his absence did make her heart grow fonder and that she had at last entered into "an advanced passionate phase of feeling for him without any obvious reason."

Amy was an excellent pianist who, as soon as they became engaged, suggested that instead of spending money on a honeymoon they buy a piano for the rectory. "I don't want to delude you with the idea that you will find me as clay in the hands of the potter," she wrote to her future husband. They were married on May 19, 1887, at St. George's Church in Montreal, but not before she shocked the community by postponing the date of the wedding so she could attend a performance of the Boston Philharmonic Orchestra. "I was hooted at by everyone as tho' I had proposed a highway robbery or something equally outrageous," she wrote. "My mind, as you will see, is beginning to take a severely practical turn."

They would have seven children: William Bridges Scott (1888) who graduated in the top of his class in Law and later became Quebec's hard-nosed Associate Chief Justice; Henry Hutton Scott (1890), who was known as Harry and was killed in World War I. Their only daughter, Mary, was born in 1892. Four boys followed: Elton (1893); Charles Lennox (1895); Francis Reginald Scott (1899), who would overshadow his father as a poet and become one of the founders of the Co-operative Commonwealth Federation (CCF), the forerunner of the New Democratic Party; and the youngest, Arthur Elliott (1901). As a father, Scott seems to be somewhat distant yet demanding. He

Miss Amy Brooks, 1885.
McCord Museum, 11-77669.

refs to "my boy," which sometimes makes it difficult to know which son in particular he is writing about. His son Elton obviously inspired his only novel, *Elton Hazelwood*, which was published in 1891. It was a dull, moralizing tome with links of chivalry to an Englishman's code of ethics. In the words of one critic, it was a book that "should pretty well be entirely rewritten." His publisher wound up giving away as many copies as were sold.

Because of his Tractarian views, Scott couldn't find work in the Montreal Diocese. One of his classmates in England was Lennox Williams, the son of the Bishop of Quebec. Through his school-tie connection with Lennox he was accepted in Quebec and assigned to St. George's in Drummondville. The rural parish, 100 kilometres east of Montreal, was founded in 1822 by British soldiers, but the stone church in a wooded glade off Heriot Street had been built in 1867. The parish welcomed him with deep misgivings about his High Church ideas. Scott informed his parishioners that as an Anglo-Catholic priest he expected to hear their confessions before he would allow them to receive communion, and created a fuss when he insisted on using communion wafers instead of bread. It is hard today to understand the depths of animosity towards his beliefs and the mistrust his uncompromising attitude engendered. Even Scott's brother, Frank, took him to task for his "Popish" aspirations. "We are all terribly grieved to hear about the row out in Drummondville," Frank wrote to him,

I thought you did not understand the people as well as you flattered yourself you did. You can't push people, you have got to lead them. For heaven's sake my dear brother, should you get over this row, let it be a lesson to you. I have grown up with you and know something about your nature and can say that there is a portion of it which is of a more undesirable type. It was that which asserted itself when you were a boy and which you nobly suppressed when you got older. This it is I am afraid which crops up occasionally and manifests itself in the stubborn bigotry which characterizes some of your actions. I can assure you that we are all deeply sorry for you, however, rest assured I will always uphold true Catholic principles, but popish rites are most abhorrent, and if they have been preached in Drummondville, I sympathize with the people.

Archdeacon Roe chastised Scott for "holding that the Catholic faith is imperiled," and suggested that Scott leave Drummondville if he couldn't hold his congregation together. His mentor, Father Wood, urged Scott not to exacerbate the conflict, and as a compromise, urged him to hold two services, "the Catholic one at an early hour, and an old fashioned one later in the day." Andrew Hunter Dunn, the fifth Bishop of Quebec, pleaded with him: "the wafer bread, the walking out in a cassock, erecting a crucifix, the eucharistic vestments, the use of the sign of the cross, genuflections, prostrations, etc..." These, Hunter Dunn insisted, could not, "be said to be essential," to Anglican worship. Even his wife Amy, was bemused. "I might almost fancy you enjoy the situation, (providing you always come out ahead)," she wrote.

By 1896 Lennox Williams was genuinely distressed to learn that after almost a decade in Drummondville, Scott had lost a significant number of his parishioners. That didn't faze Scott in the least and he continued to celebrate the Anglo-Catholic Mass daily. Even if the pews were empty for the service he delighted in reminding Williams that "the church was filled with angels." Williams did not wish to see Scott continue "antagonizing his congregation." By then Scott, too, had had enough and was considering offers to move to St.

Luke's in Toronto or to a mission district in Vancouver. Williams, instead found him a place as an assistant at St. Matthew's, the Anglo-Catholic church on St-Jean Street in Quebec City, a few blocks north of the National Assembly. The parish had been established in 1855, and the neo-gothic church building was designed by William Tutin Thomas in the 1870s. St. Matthew's had a strong outreach program, supported missionary work at home and abroad and had a nurse of its own who performed regular rounds. Scott moved into the rectory at 5 Simard Street, and on the vestry wall posted a poem about duty that was to be his guiding principle.

> Duty from the Golden Wings
> God on man his glory flings
> And all the Harps of God are strung
> With the songs that thou has sung.

Scott made headlines in October 1897 when he plunged into the St. Lawrence River to rescue a homeless drunk who had fallen from the Champlain Wharf located below Quebec's Château Frontenac. He was awarded the Royal Canadian Humane Association Medal for heroic conduct. His bishop, with the faintly superior attitude that characterized Anglicans as a group of exclusives since the Conquest, congratulated him for his bravery, especially because "he risked his life for a French Canadian."

"My Lord," Scott replied, I did it for a fellow Canadian."

Scott's first book of poetry, *A Soul's Quest*, was published in London by Kegan Paul and Trench in 1888 (although he had self-published a small collection of his own five years earlier). A third volume, *My Lattice and Other Poems*, followed in 1894. The death from typhoid that year of his younger brother, Charles 'Boots' Scott in Duluth, Minnesota during a raging storm, deeply affected him.

'Boots' had travelled west to try his hand at farming, and when that failed, found work at a bank in Duluth. Scott was with his brother and as he died glanced out of the window which overlooked Lake Superior and was inspired to write about his belief in an afterlife. "The end of (my brother's) life had come just as the storm too, had passed. I saw the morning star above the golden gates of the opening day. One's attitude towards death ought to be the promise of a larger and more glorious life, an entrance into a region of existence which our human form precludes from entering."

In October 1899 Britain sent troops to contain guerilla fighters in Transvaal and the Orange Free State who declared independence for the two Boer Republics established by expatriate Dutch farmers. For the first time Canada deployed its soldiers abroad. Scott enlisted as a chaplain with the 8th Regiment Royal Rifles, a militia unit which later was amalgamated with Les Voltigeurs de Québec. He had every intention of going with the troops to South Africa, because as one of his colleagues, Robert Renison, of Moosonee, Ontario explained, "The Christian world was heading for the Millennium, and the reserved seats would undoubtedly be for the British people." But Amy, who was pregnant with Arthur, had her hands full with two babies—Francis (later known as F.R.) and Charles Lennox. She was not about to be left alone to care for an infant and two toddlers.

Canon Scott came to national prominence on October 30, 1899, with the spellbinding sermon he delivered in Holy Trinity Cathedral to the Canadian contingent leaving for South Africa. *The Star* pronounced it "A masterpiece and the sole conversation among those who heard it"—high praise, indeed, considering Scott shared the pulpit with Sir Wilfrid Laurier. Scott took Deuteronomy as his text, 20:13, exhorting the men like knights of old, to consecrate their hearts and swords to the service of God and the British Empire. "War," he said was not being waged to crush people, "but ... to establish British law in a land where British sovereignty is claimed. We conquer. We advance. Wild lands come under our sway. Savages are subjugated for the Empire of the future, the Empire rising with the sun of a new century. Cruel and horrible as war is, if it be, as I believe a dreaded necessity, there surely could not be a cause worthier of the enthusiasm of a great people than the giving of light, liberty and religious tolerance not only to those oppressed in the Transvaal, but in the end, to the oppressors themselves. You are the pioneers of a new era in history. In the pause before the battle charge, during lonely sleepless nights you will feel that in life and death the eternal God is our refuge and underneath are the everlasting arms that will thrust out the enemy for us. Surely if we go forth firmly, fearlessly and mercifully to fight, we can, like Israel of old, feel that the eternal God is our refuge."

Scott soon became a commanding figure on the streets of Quebec City. "Quebecers of all religious persuasions tended to call upon him for help," writes Sandra Djwa. "He looked and to some degree acted like a Roman Catholic priest. He was fond of wearing a long black ecclesiastical cape, he displayed the crucifix, he had a habit of dropping into Roman Catholic churches as he explained to his children 'to smell the incense'. He loved the ritual of the Mass, the gilt of the statues, the holy water ...".

Queen Victoria died in 1901. Scott gave a moving eulogy which was covered by all the major newspapers of the day. Although the sun of a new century had risen and ushered in a new Edwardian era Scott remained tied to the conventions of the 19th century.

While Scott was away on a papal visit to Pius X in Rome his nine year old son, Charles Lennox, died of pneumonia on October 13, 1904. Scott never forgave himself for being absent and expressed his anguish in the poem "My Little Son."

My little son, my little son, he calls to me forever
    Across the gulfs and through the mists which shroud
        him from my sight

I hear him in the noonday, in the midst of all the
turmoil
I hear him, oh, so plainly in the silence of the night ...

In 1906 Scott was appointed Canon at Holy Trinity Cathedral. The following year he had a sanctuary lamp installed in St. Matthew's which, in Roman Catholic churches, signals the presence of the consecrated host in the tabernacle. He aped the Roman Catholic custom of 40 hours of devotion, which bemused some in his congregation. In spite of the objections Scott kept the lamp burning, insist-ing that when it came to the Eucharist, "no splendor of decorative ritual can be inappropriate." He wrote and staged *Key of Life*, an eminently forgettable mystery play about the seven deadly sins, which he dedicated to Edmund Wood.

When Quebec City celebrated the Tercentenary of its founding by Samuel de Champlain in 1608, Scott was part of the pageantry and was inducted into the Royal Society of Canada and was regarded as the city's poet laureate. The floridly patriotic nine-verse ode he composed for the occasion was "Canada," which begins:

Out of the clouds of Time's horizon, dawneth the new
    Day, spacious and fair:
    White-winged over the world it shineth; wide-winged
        over the land and sea
Spectres and ghosts of battles and hatred flee at the touch
    of the morning air:
    Throned on the ocean, the new Sun ariseth; Darkness
        is over, we wake, and are free
Ages of ages guarded and tended mountain and waterfall,
    river and plain,
    Forests that sighed with the sorrows of God in the
        infinite
    night when the stars looked down ...

Frederick's and Amy's seven children.
Studio portrait, Quebec City, 1904, just before Charles's death
at age nine.
Back row: William, Mary; middle row: Elton, Frank, Harry;
front row: Charles, Arthur.
Courtesy of Stephen S. Kelley.

He was forty-seven years old. Half of his life was over. He had earned a reputation as a minor poet of some renown, the author of a hymn, "Cast Thy Care on Jesus" (Make him now thy friend), and might have been content to remain a vicar at St. Matthew's, preoccupied with synod meetings, sermons and ministering to the underprivileged. But with a fatal assassin's bullet fired in Sarajevo on June 28, 1914, the course of his life changed.

Chapter Two

EVERYONE KNEW THAT WAR with Germany was imminent but no one knew when it would begin or what excuse would be used to start it. And once it began, there was no way that Canada could avoid being drawn into it. When England went to war, the entire Empire was automatically at war. In anticipation of hostilities, The Minister of the Militia, Sam Hughes, promised to raise a Canadian contingent of 20,000 volunteers. On July 31, 1914, four days before the "War to End All Wars" began in Europe, Scott, now fifty-three years old, telephoned Hughes and offered his services to the Canadian Expeditionary Force. Then he went home to tell his startled wife, Amy, that he had volunteered because "some mysterious power" was dragging him "into a whirlpool." Bound by fierce patriotism and convinced that "war was the natural ambition of men," he earnestly believed that the very foundations of British civilization were at stake. Taking his cue from Matthew 10:16 he saw himself as "a sheep in the midst of wolves...as wise as a serpent and as harmless as a dove."

Although he was a High Church Anglican, Scott did not stake his faith on denominational dogma alone. He had faith in the spirit of God, in the truth revealed in the gospel narratives free from the trappings of organized religion. His philosophy may best be contained in his verse, "Catholicism."

> Down the dim lit glades of time
> Age after age, things divers blend,
> Each working for the same great end

And in its working each sublime
Was it in vain that Buddha taught
Or that Mohammed lived and died?
Have they not, working side by side
In different climes God's purpose wrought?

Even people without theology, who profess no creed, or even pretend to be indifferent when it comes to religion, are, he wrote, "unalterably fixed in faith, if they subscribe to the greatest com-mandment: Love one another." More than twenty-five years in the priesthood had taught him that a sermon delivered with reason, humour, and emotion which reflected a depth of character could not only rally the troops, but be of comfort to the wounded and the dying.

His son, William, enlisted the day after his father. The two of them spent a month being conditioned for war at Valcartier, a chaotic military training camp being built from scratch in the wilderness 25 kilometres northwest of Quebec City. Mobilizing the army took weeks. Thousands of volunteers caught up by the excitement of war arrived by train from across the county and marched from a nearby railway siding into the chaos of a camp which was still under construction. A cinema was opened but mysteriously burned after the men complained that it kept showing the same film over and over. He was issued a private's uniform and his first assignment as chaplain was to preside over the funeral of a recruit who had committed suicide, a dismal service conducted in the woods at night in dripping rain. As a chaplain, Scott held the rank of a commissioned officer and was therefore entitled to a batman, or personal valet. He selected a theological student from Ontario as his assistant because he liked the young man's apparent piety. Scott lived to regret his choice.

I found afterwards, it is unwise to select a batman for their piety. The man I chose was a failure as a batman. When

(*Left to right*) Frank, Amy Brooks Scott, Constance Hall Scott (Harry's wife), Harry (with Arthur in front) and Mrs. Hall (Harry's mother-in-law), circa 1914. *Courtesy of Stephen S. Kelley.*

some duty had been neglected, and I reprimanded him, he would say, 'Would you like me to recite Browning?' He nearly exterminated me once by setting a stone water bottle to heat on my stove without unscrewing the stopper. The steam blew out with a terrific force, and filled the tent. A moment or two later, it would have exploded with disastrous consequences. I would have been killed—an unworthy end for one about to fight the greatest war the world has ever known. He only smiled faintly, and asked if I should like to hear him recite some poetry.

As Scott inspected the camp he was apprehensive. "I had an impression that we were a rather awkward squad neither fish, flesh or fowl."

Still, England had won every war that it had fought in living memory, and everyone expected this one would be over in six months; two years at the most. Scott wasn't confident that a rag-tag fighting force of farmers, university students, clerks and the unemployed could "meet and overthrow the trained legions of Germany." He went through a period of "anxious thought and deep foreboding" but concluded that he "belonged to a race which has never been conquered. Above all, right, and therefore, God was on our side." Sam Hughes did "not believe in chaplains" and was reluctant to appoint any. When he finally agreed to let thirty-three accompany the troops, he advised them that "windy sermons would be a mistake," and that all he expected his chaplains to do was "to befriend the boys."

Two weeks before the scheduled departure Scott preached to 15,000 men at the church parade attended by the Governor General, the Duke of Connaught, his wife, Princess Patricia, and Prime Minister Robert Borden. He took as his text Matthew 10:39:

"He that lays down his life for my sake shall find it," reminding the men that they were "champions of a noble cause." On September 28, he sailed to England aboard the Cunard Liner, *Andania*, with half of the men of the 14th Battalion from Westmount, and with the 16th Scottish Battalion from Vancouver. They left in high spirits, cheerfully prepared to support the Mother Country in need. Each morning at 5:30, pipers would march through the ship to wake everyone up. On one occasion, some men assigned to the 14th Battalion were so irritated by the skirl they turned the hoses on the pipers. Scott befriended the wireless operator, and received daily reports of what was happening in Europe. The news was not especially encouraging. There was word of a "retreating and broken British army" at Mons where the British forces met the Germans for the first time. Scott had been sworn to secrecy and could not let any of the men know that heavy British losses meant immediate reinforcements were needed. All Scott knew of war was what he had read in books. He had cast himself as a Christian knight, off on a glorious crusade. He wrote "Blood Guilt" as a battle cry.

> The brand of Cain is on your brow, Emperor!
> A crown of gold may hide it now, Emperor!
> But when the day of reckoning comes,
> . . .
> A people's wrath will rend the skies
> And topple down your dynasties, Emperor!

As Scott neared England, he began to question his courage. "I knew that if an ordinary officer on running away under fire would get the sympathy of a large number of people who would say 'the poor fellow has shell shock.' But if a chaplain were to run away, 600 men would say at once, 'we have no more use for religion.'"

The convoy arrived at Plymouth on October 14, 1914 and the expeditionary forces boarded the train to Patney, and from there marched to Salisbury Plain near Stonehenge. But the "glamour of romance and chivalry" that Scott expected was swept away almost from the instant he arrived by the worst winter in living memory. "The gales of heaven swept over the plain, tents were blown down. The rains descended, the floods came and the storm beat upon the tents, and the tents which were old and thin were blown away," he wrote. "The green sward was soon trampled into deep and clinging mud. In some places the mud was so deep it went over the top of my rubber boots. The weather was so bad that a route march meant a lot of wet soldiers with nowhere to dry their clothes upon the return." His son Harry, who was articling with a Montreal law firm, commiserated with his father. "I think the Riviera would have been more comfortable—provided you were in easy reach of Monte Carlo," Harry joked in a letter. "Well Old Man, keep well and write some more poetry about your friend the Kaiser."

Scott and another chaplain attempted to boost morale by putting on a variety show for the men in the YMCA tent. Just as the program began, "like the fall of the walls of Jericho at the sound of Joshua's trumpets, a mighty gale struck, and with a ripping sound the whole thing collapsed. On another occasion, the paymaster's tent blew away as he was paying off the battalion. The five shilling notes flew over the Plains like birds over the sea. The men quickly chased them and gathered them up and on finding them stained with mud found it unnecessary to return them."

On another night, the huge marquee above the tent in which Harrod's had opened a mess for a large number of officers, blew down just as Scott sat down to eat and he had to "forage in the various canteens for tinned salmon and packages of biscuits." There was no alcohol available at the training camp so many of the

Canadians invaded the local pubs where they created havoc in the surrounding villages.

The first Christmas overseas was celebrated in Amesbury Abbey, a 13th-century Benedictine shrine known as the Abbey of St. Mary and St. Melor. None of the soldiers knew how much longer they would be kept on the Plain, or when they might be sent to the Front. As Scott put it, "life was certainly a puzzle. Why were we being kept there? When were we going to leave? Why were we not wanted in France?" Men started dying of meningitis. Early in the New Year as conditions on Salisbury Plain continued to deteriorate the Canadians increasingly felt that their efforts were being ignored by the Imperial War Office, who, in reality, regarded them as little more than "a mob of hot blooded amateurs." Boredom set in. The men became unruly. There were fist fights, drunken brawls and desertions. Discipline became a problem. Even Scott conceded that the conduct of many of the soldiers was "indeed disgraceful...but with reason."

Lieutenant Colonel Francis B. Ware, D.S.O., a friend of Scott's who commanded the 7th Regiment Fusiliers of London (Ontario) during the war (and later the 12th Military District in Regina) acknowledged that the division "was rapidly acquiring a rather bad name because of the misdemeanours of many who simply walked away from their units. After twenty-one days the men were declared deserters, and as every unit was over strength, commanding officers were glad to be rid of such undesirables. In all fairness," Ware wrote in an unpublished manuscript, "the majority of the deserters were not native-born Canadians but immigrants from the British Isles who used the Canadian Expeditionary Force as a means of getting back to the Old Country where many of them ultimately joined British regiments." Even more troubling, a number of the Canadians were found to be unfit for active service. As Clifford Wells, a lieutenant

Scott, Salisbury Plain, England, 1915.
Photograph by A.R. Bott, McCord Museum, MP-1982.64.72.

from Westmount observed, "The proportion of Canadians here who are marked unfit for active service is disgracefully large. It is a great mistake for anyone to enlist if his health is not sufficiently good for him to endure the hardships of active service. It is a waste of his own time and of the Government's money."

Scott was still in England when he was gratified to learn that the weight of his position, which he had used to denounce an anti-Semitic attack against a Jewish merchant in Quebec City, had paid off. Four years earlier, Jacques-Edouard Plamondon had given a speech and distributed a pamphlet which accused Jews of endangering the Roman Catholic faith. Shortly afterwards Quebec City's synagogue was vandalized, and the windows of a shop owned by Benjamin Ortenberg were smashed in a wave of violence. Ortenberg launched a libel action which dragged through the courts for years. Initially the courts dismissed the suit on the grounds that Plamondon did not specifically refer to Ortenberg. Scott wrote letters in support of the Jews in Quebec City, which at the time numbered less than a hundred. Ortenberg appealed, and at the end of December, 1914, was awarded damages. "Evidently your evidence was a strong point in the appeal court's decision," his son Harry informed his father of the news in a letter. "Prayers are probably being offered for your safety in the synagogues through the city."

It wasn't until February 1915 that Scott learned the troops were about to be deployed to France, but that only five chaplains would be allowed to go with them. Those that had been selected were instructed to invoke the name of the Holy Spirit only to stimulate the patriotic spirit. A third of the volunteers in the expeditionary force were Anglican, one in five identified as Roman Catholic, one in five as Presbyterian, one in ten were Methodists, and the rest from other denominations. While most of them identified with a specific denomination, the British High Command reasoned that soldiers were generally indifferent to religion. As Peter Hanson explains in *Muddling Through*, his book about the organization of the British Army Chaplaincy, "a unified command structure for chaplains had been created for the Canadian Expeditionary Force, but a lack of experience, internal politics and difficulties in communications between churches in Europe and in Canada led to an unsatisfactory state of affairs for much of the war." The number of chaplains allowed to go to France, therefore, was restricted and the directive further spelled out that once they got there they were prohibited from going anywhere near the front lines. The involvement of chaplains with the fighting men was complex. Although chaplains were commissioned into the army, they were subject to military rules and regulations, standard operating procedures, and incredibly detailed orders which often put a chokehold on the way a number of religious communities carried out their ministry. The precise role of the chaplain remained a work in progress. For example, although they were commissioned officers, they had no authority. Scott, who "took his marching orders from God," resented many of the restrictions, especially the rule that kept him away from the Front lines. But the commanding Chaplain General, Llewellyn Gwynne, Archbishop of Khartoum, pointed out that Lord Kitchener had specifically ordered the Canadians to bring only five chaplains with them and they had ignored the rules by sending thirty-three. He further pointed out that if thirty-three Canadian chaplains were not able to control the "disgraceful, disorderly conduct" of many of the Canadian soldiers he didn't think religion was going to make a difference.

"Think of how much worse the men would have been if there had only been five chaplains instead of thirty-three," countered Scott.

Eventually eleven Canadian chaplains were permitted to accompany the troops, but because of his age, Scott was not one of them.

Gwynne did not think so old a man could bear the "rough and tumble of the heaviest fighting in history." Scott was assigned, instead, to report to Number 2 General Hospital. Since no one told him precisely where Number 2 Hospital was located (but knowing full well it was in nearby Lavington, on the northern edge of Salisbury Plain in Wiltshire), he disingenuously deduced that Number 1 General Hospital *had* to be in England. So he would have to go to France to find Number 2 General Hospital.

Chapter Three

SCOTT FELT HE HAD BEEN DEALT "a great blow" by not being deployed with the Canadians. Nevertheless, he remained relentlessly optimistic about the war and about the role he would play in it. He was determined to share the danger with the combatants and was not about to sit out the war in England. Believing that "the Lord would provide," he made up his mind to stow away on the *City of Chester*, a steamship bound for France which had been pressed into service as a troop ship. On February 13, 1915, the evening before it was scheduled to sail, Canon Scott diligently performed his priestly duties in his hotel room where he baptized a sergeant. "I had a little table prepared with a white cloth and an altar cross on it. I used the chalice as a font. It was very touching, for the poor fellow was definitely earnest," he wrote to Amy.

The next morning he and his son Willie boarded the ship with the 3rd Artillery Brigade. In his unpublished memoir, Major Francis Ware, who befriended Scott at Valcartier, tells how the padre managed to get on board.

On the day of the sailing, the gallant canon appeared on the docks of Avonmouth. He had a somewhat shambling, lurching walk, that frequently caused those who didn't know him well to think that he had perhaps been imbibing a bit too frequently. Giving his kit to a friend to carry on board, and weighed down by a mass of haversacks, water bottles, maps, hymn books and everything else he could carry, he started up the steep gangway, his face wreathed in a great smile." All of this—the walk, the trappings, the silly grin, attracted the attention of the officer in command who suspected Scott was drunk.

"How do you do sir," the officer greeted Scott.

"Very well sir," came the cheerful reply.

"Who are you?" the officer asked.

"Why, I am Number 2 General Hospital," Scott declared.

Believing Scott to be intoxicated and "feeling that it would not be safe to let an officer in that condition wander around the decks alone," he let him board. The irony is that Scott was a teetotaller active in the Temperance Movement. He frowned upon soldiers drinking and instead of dispensing the padre's rum rations, he would often pass out temperance cards, suggesting the men take the pledge instead of the ration.

Once aboard, Scott found the vessel so horribly crowded that he was forced to sleep on a table in the saloon. The ship hit heavy seas which caused Scott to roll off the table and land on top of a sleeping medic, crushing him and "squeezing from him some wonderfully religious expressions." When they reached St-Nazaire Scott had "a good sleep in a comfortable hotel," and the next morning left for the Front. He had been in France once before, in 1883, when he went to visit the 13th-century cathedral in Amiens. Once again he was reminded that "it was a great thing to be travelling in that country of romance and chivalry."

One week after leaving Salisbury Plain Scott arrived in Haze-brouck, a market town in Flanders, where a brigadier lent him a horse. He rode to Caëstre where he was delighted to be invited to spend the night with the mayor's family. He turned down an offer to climb aboard a water truck and drive the 20 kilometres to

Armentières because he wanted the men to know "their parson could rough it." Being a canon, he quipped, he thought it was appropriate that he march with the machine-gun section. To avoid detection, he preferred to travel by night. One evening, as he made his way along in the dark, he inadvertently fell into a latrine, and had to clean himself with "water almost as ill-savoured as the pool itself." Then as he stumbled along, he was challenged by a sentry. He hadn't a clue what the password was. The only thing that saved him from being shot was "the white gleam of my clerical collar which, on this account, I had frequently thought of painting with luminous paint." He arrived in Armentières on the evening of February 14, to discover it had already been in the hands of the Germans. The church and city hall had been shelled, the clock on the city hall stopped at five minutes to twelve. As he arrived he was welcomed by Imperial chaplain Harry Blackburne, who was in the middle of preparing three men about to face a firing squad at dawn. One of them, twenty-year-old George Collins of the 1st Battalion Lincolnshire Regiment, was to be executed for cowardice, and the other two, Private Richard Morgan and Line Corporal William Price, both with the 2nd Battalion Welsh Regiment, for the murder of their overbearing platoon sergeant, Hughie Hayes. Collins had only been in France for five weeks when he was detailed for service in the trenches. Instead of reporting for duty he deserted his unit and went to Paris where he drank himself into a stupor. When arrested he claimed he remembered nothing. A military court martial pronounced him guilty of cowardice. As an example to the men he was sentenced to be shot at dawn. The day after he was executed at Loker in West Flanders, headquarters circulated a memo suggesting that in future "good fighting men not be shot for absence arising out of a drunken spree." Scott shuddered at the "hideous" experience, not knowing that before war's end, he too, would have to prepare a soldier for execution.

In Armentières Scott was given a room in a school that had been bombed and had a number of its windows blown out. "I must not say where I am," he wrote to assure Amy that he had arrived in France and was well. "Picture me sitting in a little dirty yellow-papered room with religious pictures of the usual French-Canadian sort and crucifixes on the wall. My window looks out on the paved courtyard now filled with our horses and mules all tied in rows. The bright spring sunlight is pouring in my window, and every now and then the roar of a huge gun is heard in the distance…it is like a glorious thunderstorm in the lower St. Lawrence."

It was spring in Flanders and Scott was wonderfully responsive to the season. "The grass was green, the trees and hedgerows were full of sap, and the buds ready to burst into new life. As one walked down the roads in the bright sunshine and smelled the fresh winds bearing the scent of springtime, an exquisite feeling of delight filled the soul." He also ate well: "the food is excellent, such coffee, omelettes and chocolate. They call me Monsieur L'Aumonier."

As he held his first church service in Europe in the local hos-pital, the town was shelled, and two houses blown away. When he attended a church parade the following Sunday, "the general commanding ordered the men with good sight to be posted on the look-out for aeroplanes. It was funny to have men watching for aeroplanes while we were at service," he wrote. "The sky is clear and beautiful. I am so glad to be here. Everyone is so kind and good. Our men are behaving splendidly."

Although the countryside was pitch black at night he was able to find his way around by the light of "the full moon, which now pours down such wonderful silver on the lonely, battered brick streets." As he caught up with the Royal Montreal Regiment on its way to the reserve trenches at Wieltje, Belgium for the Second Battle of Ypres, he ran into Brigade Major John Nicol Warmington who demanded to know what in hell Scott was doing in France.

"What unit are you attached to?" Warmington asked.

"Why, Number 2 General Hospital," Scott replied.

"Where is it?"

"Why, I don't really know. I've come to France to find it."

Warmington peered at him. "You know very well it is in Lavington. On Salisbury Plain. In England."

Fortunately, Scott was ordered to report to General Edwin Alderson and await further instructions. Alderson was an aging but experienced general who had commanded the Canadians in the South African war. He had been touted to become Canada's Governor General, but instead accepted an appointment as Queen Victoria's aide-de-camp. When the Queen died Alderson was promoted to major general and sent to India to command the 6th (Poona) Division. Upon his return, he had hoped to retire as Master of Foxhounds in the South Shropshire Hunt. But because he had worked with Canadians in South Africa, when the war began he was put in charge of the First Canadian Division. Scott walked the seven kilometres to the general's headquarters at Strazeele. Perhaps because of his soft spot for Canadians, Alderson told Scott he could stay in France but warned him to stay 65 kilometres away from the trenches. If he went any closer to the front lines he would immediately be sent back to England. Scott was assigned a batman by the name of Murdoch MacDonald, "a proper young highlander carrying a rifle with a fixed bayonet on his shoulder," and was given a mud plastered cottage at Sailly-sur-la-Lys. He fitted up one of the rooms as a chapel, chalked the words CHAPLAIN on the door, and was in business.

With that, he immediately left for the trenches.

We reached a communication trench with bits of wood on the bottom of it. We passed by a row of muddy soldiers to a weird little dug out in which four of us squeezed. A candle was burning and there was a box of hand grenades. We had a most delicious supper, served under the most primitive conditions. After supper I went to bed and slept on a shelf— a little dugout in the mud with a corrugated iron roof and straw for walls and a floor. One officer lent me a blanket but it was chilly, so I did not sleep very well and the banging of the artillery and cracking of the German rifles beside the firing of our own rifles kept up sort of a cradle song that was not always conducive to sleep, although I must confess it was delicious to lie in the little straw covered bunk and feel that at last we were in the real thing.... When we woke in the morning it was very foggy. On account of the fog the Major would not let us have a public service. The fog hides the sound of the approaching enemy as well as the sight. However, in the little bug hutch we had Holy Communion and six received. We were so crowded I did not stand up straight. The table was covered with an illustrated paper and we were all muddy and dirty. Only two could kneel at a time, but it was most impressive. The crack of the bullets overhead and the singing of those that ricocheted was very frequent."

He was immensely pleased with himself, and as he wrote to Amy, "even if I had been found out and shipped back, I at least had seen the trenches." His first glimpse of calamity came later that day when he witnessed two men hit by sniper fire. One day soon afterwards, as he was going into the dugouts at Ploegstreet, he saw General Alderson approaching down the road. To avoid the general he ducked into an orchard behind a farm house where he surprised a battery of British soldiers who weren't expecting to see a chaplain. When Scott explained he was hiding from a general, the men applauded. "I made up my mind that if I wished to live through the war three things had to be avoided—sentries, cesspools and Generals. They are all sources of special danger."

Two weeks later he ventured from the reserve trenches into No Man's Land, the strip of ground between a meandering network of opposing trenches that stretched for 700 kilometres from Ostend, Belgium, to Basel, Switzerland. He went to Houplines, east of Armentières, for formal instruction in trench warfare, and in a letter home blithely likened the "novelty of sporadic gunfire" to a war being fought in a children's nursery. "The Germans occasionally open machine guns on the fields as the men are coming in at night. The men march in single file and if they have time they fall flat as the machine-guns fire." German snipers occasionally had Scott as their target. One evening as he left the trenches and walked back to town in the moonlight he had his "Macintosh cape on as it was cold and I suppose it made a sort of light mark in the moonlight, for I heard a bullet whistle by me. I at once undid the cape and took it off and became more or less invisible." On another occasion, while looking through a periscope, a bullet narrowly missed the periscope. "I moved away," Scott commented dryly, "in order to save the instrument from being damaged." Although Scott had been shot at he was, in the early days of the war, still ambivalent about being killed.

"You have no idea what fascination danger has for me," he wrote his wife on March 1. "I would not be back in Canada now while the war is going on for anything. Almost every day, some are wounded, some are killed ..."

Then someone he knew, one of his son's companions, Richard Carter Eaton, a twenty-three-year-old clerk from Montreal, was badly wounded. "A bullet struck him in the mouth and after knocking out his front teeth went round and put out his eye and perhaps lodged in his brain," Scott informed Amy. "When he was wounded he called for Willie and he held his hand for a long time. Willie was very much affected and wanted to carry him out of the trench in the day time, but he was not allowed. It meant certain death to them all. Captain Frost says Willie was splendid."

While making his way through the muddy trenches Scott encountered an officer whom he mistook for a colonel. It was, in fact, a General—Walter Norris Congreve, Commander of the 13th British Army Corps who had been awarded a Victoria Cross during the Boer War. Scott was certain he would be reprimanded and sent back to England, but Congreve invited him for lunch "at infantry headquarters in a fine château." Congreve tried to impress upon Scott the dangers of trench warfare, and politely but firmly insisted that Scott quit the trenches. As an aside Congreve added that if he could press a button and annihilate every German from the face of the earth he would do so. At the time, Scott was shocked at Congreve's savagery. Later, he would say that he too, had spent "four years looking for that button." On March 10, as the first British offensive of the war—the Battle of Neuve Chapelle—began, Scott was safely at Laventrie. Although Neuve Chapelle was wrested from the enemy the overall assault failed, and had to be abandoned because of a lack of artillery. It was, in the words of one general, "a tactical success which led to nothing." Among the mangled bodies of the wounded that were brought back in ambulances, was Scott's son, William, who had lost an eye in the fighting. For the first time Scott began to appreciate the real danger he was in. Willie was taken to England for treatment and Scott saw him off in a hospital train at Merville. As Canon Scott then returned to Neuve Chapelle to conduct funeral rites for the dead he passed a brick shrine with a large white crucifix inside. As he looked at it in the moonlight, a German flare went up, illuminating it.Scott wrote the first of his war poems, "On the Rue du Bois," which appeared in the London Times on April 21, 1915.

Oh pallid Christ within this broken shrine,
Now those torn Hands and not that heart of Thine
Have given the nations blood to drink like wine.

Through weary years and neath the changing skies,
Men turned their back on those appealing Eyes
And scorned as vain Thine awful sacrifice.

Kings with their armies, children in their play,
Have passed unheeding down this shell-ploughed way,
The great world knew not where its true strength lay.

In pomp and luxury, in lust of gold,
In selfish ease, in pleasures manifold,
"Evil is good, good evil," we were told.

Yet here, where nightly the great flare-lights gleam,
And murder stalks triumphant in their beam,
The world has wakened from its empty dream.

At last, O Christ, in this strange, darkened land,
Where ruined homes lie round on every hand,
Life's deeper truths men come to understand.

For lonely graves along the country side,
Where sleep those brave hearts who for others died,
Tell of life's union with the Crucified.

And new light kindles in the mourner's eyes
Like day dawn breaking through the rifted skies
For life is born of life's self-sacrifice.

At nearby Laventrie he converted a large barn "full of beautiful yellow straw," into a church. At Easter he celebrated Mass at Estaires in a hall which had once been used as a cinema, which he was able to make "bright and churchlike amid the sordid surroundings." It was an unusually solemn service considering the occasion. "It was the first Easter spent away from home, and many knew it could be the last Easter they might celebrate on earth," he explained. Following the service, fifteen thousand men gathered in the town square to hear the Bishop of London, Arthur Winnington-Ingram, bless the troops and remind them, as if they needed to be reminded, that they were about to embark on a vital battle.

Instead of remaining with his brigade Scott went off to Ypres to visit St. Martin's Cathedral, and the 16th-century seigneurial Château Balloy at Terdeghem. He remarked on its twin facades—one typically French, the other typically Flemish. He returned to Estaires in the dark, got lost, and seeing a white shadowy figure, began to ask it for instructions, explaining that he had lost his way and was looking for his unit. He rambled on for several minutes before it dawned on him that he had been talking to a plaster statue of some unknown saint. As a means of calming his nerves, he began composing poems in his head, often reciting them aloud as he walked along. One evening, after he had been assigned to spend a night with several officers in a small, dirty farmhouse near Sailly-sur-la-Lys, he decided instead to go for a walk through the darkened village and, with his wounded son "Willum" in mind, composed "A Canadian," a poem which he dedicated to Amy as a 28th wedding anniversary present.

> The glad and brave young heart
> Had come across the sea,
> He longed to play his part
> In crushing tyranny.
>
> The mountains and plains
> Of his beloved land
> Were wine within his veins
> And gave an iron hand.

He scorned the thought of fear,
    He murmured not at pain,
The call of God was clear,
    The path of duty plain.

Beneath the shower of lead
    Of poison and of fire,
He charged and fought and bled,
    Ablaze with one desire.

O Canada, with pride,
    Look up and greet the morn,
Since of thy wounded side
    Such breed of men is born.

Horace Smith-Dorrien, the tweedy British general who had been instrumental in getting Scott's poem, *On the Rue du Bois*, published in *The Times*, came to Estaires to inspect the Canadian troops. Smith-Dorrien had been one of the few British officers who had survived the Battle of Isandlwana in South Africa in 1879, but as the general who led two divisions into the first major battle of the war at Mons, had been forced to retreat. Eight months of trench warfare had resulted in a deadlock, and the war was becoming one of exhaustion. The Canadian Division was about to replace the French. Smith-Dorrien had been told that while the Canadians were efficient they were not combat hardened and wouldn't be able to stand their ground. Smith-Dorrien wanted to know whether Scott thought the Canadians were ready to be fed into battle. Naively, Scott boasted that the one thing the Canadians could be counted upon would be to "hold their ground." Scott moved to the Ypres Salient, Belgium, with the Canadian troops in preparation for what would be their first real test of the war. On Sunday, April 18, as Scott was conducting a service at Ypres, he had a premonition that "big things were going to happen."

The Germans held the high ground around the city and were able to bombard it from the east, the north and the south. Although the Canadians were technically under the command of General Edwin Alderson, command at the brigade level was in the hands of inexperienced soldiers whose only military training had been with the Canadian militia. To make matters worse they were armed with defective Ross Rifles and less than serviceable Colt machine guns. The German barrage began on April 22, 1916. As blast after deafening blast tore apart a large building in the centre of Ypres, Scott went to assess the damage and found mangled bodies in the debris. He had no time to minister to the wounded, because he heard "a ripping sound followed by a terrible explosion," as the enemy continued to lob 17-inch shells indiscriminately at ten-minute intervals into the heart of Ypres. "There was something uncanny about the arrival of shells out of the clear sky. They seemed to be things supernatural," Scott recalled. The craters made by the 17-inch shells were monstrous in size. One was no less than thirty-nine feet across and fifteen feet deep. As he looked into it he had the same sort of "eerie feeling" which he had experienced when he looked into the crater of Vesuvius. As he surveyed the damage, there was another explosion which knocked him off his feet. It all happened so fast he didn't know whether he had thrown himself down to the ground or had been blown down. He got up and sought refuge in a large chapel that was being used as a hospital. When he stepped inside he found it deserted, "rows of neat beds on each side, but not a living soul to be seen." As he made his way through the empty building another bomb exploded and all the windows in the chapel were shattered. As he ran for cover, he stumbled into a room in the church used as a guardroom. There he found a sentry, and three or four soldiers, one of whom was hiding under a wooden bench. Scott tried to cheer them up by telling them that it was unlikely another shell would hit the same building: "I remembered reading that an officer in the Navy saved his life by always sticking his head through the hole in the side of a ship made by a cannon ball," reasoning that the chance of another cannon ball hit the same place twice was a million to one."

The following morning more than a hundred soldiers and civilians lay dead in the streets.

With the approval of the town, Major Scott held the burial service for a Canadian in an open field next to the prison. The area was hastily turned into a graveyard known as Plain d'Amour, which is now usually referred to as the Middle Prison Cemetery.

As he conducted more burials, Scott experienced what he described as the most awful moment of his life: It occurred to him that England was going to lose the war. Ypres was being evacuated. People began pouring out of the city. When Scott wanted to know what was happening someone on the street told him that "the Germans are on our heels, it is a general retreat."

When Scott asked an officer to confirm that the troops were indeed retreating, he couldn't get a straight answer, but was sharply reprimanded for using the word "retreat."

"Well, if it isn't a retreat, I need to know," Scott replied. "I have to return to my lines or I will be shot for desertion."

"Never use the word retreat. We are not retreating. We are straightening the line."

As he headed east out of the city down the road through St. Jean on the way to Wieltje, one of the soldiers who was equally in the dark, asked. "Where are we going sir?"

"That," Scott quipped, "may depend on the kind of lives you have led."

They arrived in Wieltje just as the Germans released 150 tons of chlorine on the retreating army. Chlorine is a heavy, suffocating gas. To inhale it is similar to drowning. Adam Hochschild vividly describes the horror in his book, *To End All Wars*:

The spring leaves just coming out of the trees shriveled; grass turned yellow and metal green. Birds fell from the air, and chickens, pigs and cows writhed in agony and died, their bodies rotting and bloating. The even fatter rats that normally swarmed through the trenches keeping men awake by running over them in the dark on the way to feast on soldier's corpses, themselves died by the thousands.

"What they endured, no living tongue can tell," Scott wrote. Rather than leave the men, Scott decided to minister to them, even if it meant being taken prisoner of war. In his pocket was a scathing poem he had written about the Kaiser, and he was advised to tear it up as a precaution. He did as he was told, but wasn't happy about it. "I don't mind being shot or hanged," he chuckled, "but if I am, who will write the poems of war?"

Canon Scott was in the thick of the night-time counter attack in what has become known as the Battle of Kitcheners' Woods. "It was a thrilling moment, an awful and wonderful time, our field batteries never slackened as the woods echoed with the crackle of gunfire," he wrote. During the charge, shrapnel tore the back of the skull from James McNiff Duffy, a twenty-three-year-old marathon man with the 16th Battalion. Duffy had been born in Ireland, took up long-distance running in Scotland, and after moving to Hamilton, Ontario represented Canada in the 1912 Games of the V Olympiad in Stockholm, Sweden. He went on to win seven consecutive marathons, including the 1914 Boston Marathon. Scott attempted to assist Duffy only to discover "his brain was protruding." In his memoirs, Scott was defiant.

The angel of death was passing down, and prevented the Germans from gaining ground. Gun flashes lit up the horizon but above us the moon and stars looked quietly down. It was an awful and wonderful time. Wonderful deeds of heroism were done by our men along those shell ploughed fields. In spite of the enemy's immense numeric superiority and his brutal launching of poisonous gas, he did not get through.

As bullets cracked against brick walls, Scott made his way to the dressing station crowded with men suffering from the effects of the poison gas. There he found "an old woman like the face of the witch of Endor, apparently unmoved by anything that was happening, grinding coffee in a mill and making a black concoction which she sold to the men." Early in the morning, Ypres was in flames, "there was a tremendous noise of guns now at the Front," and orders were given to evacuate the dressing station. Scott was prepared to stay behind with the wounded who could not be moved and risk being taken prisoner of war. "I was in good health and the Germans treated chaplains, when they took them prisoners, very kindly," he wrote.

Told he was needed at the 3rd Infantry Brigade Headquarters down the road at a place called Shell Trap Farm, Scott went to the moated farm house only to find another makeshift dressing station filled to overflowing. There, he assisted Frank, "Scrimmy" Scrimger, a young doctor from McGill, who was "working away like a Trojan. The operating room was a veritable shambles. The doctor had his shirt sleeves rolled up and his hands and arms covered in blood." Scott began distributing communion to the wounded and the dying lying in the straw, "and took down messages which they were sending to their relatives at home." The dressing station soon became so crowded with casualties that the medics had to take over a nearby church.

The men were lying on rows on the cold stone floor. It was a strange scene, the wounded were laid out, some on the floor, some on chairs, and some waiting for the ambulance that was to take them back to the base. In the distance we heard the roar of the battle, and here in the dim light of the hollow-sounding aisles were shadowy figures huddled together. I thought it might help the men to have a talk with them, so I told them what a noble part they had played in holding back the German advance. I held a short service, and they all joined in the Lord's Prayer. It was most impressive, in that large dim church to hear the voices, not loudly, but quite distinctly repeating the words from different parts of the building. After the Lord's Prayer I said, 'Boys, the curé won't mind your smoking cigarettes in church tonight, so I am going to pass round some cigarettes.' I had a box of 500 which had been sent to me.

As he was in the church, the Shell Trap Farm field hospital was hit by what was almost certainly friendly fire from a plane with Allied markings. Dr. Scrimger ordered the building evacuated. During the evacuation, Scrimger risked his life to save a patient, and for his heroism would be awarded the Victoria Cross.

While the attack was underway Scott circled back to his lodgings in Ypres, now the most ravaged city in Europe. Shelled on three sides, he found "the lovely city was lit up in flames," its famous Cloth Hall and Cathedral in ruins. His batman, Murdoch McDonald, was waiting for him. Scott insisted on breakfast being served. "Fancy having breakfast while the town is being shelled." McDonald looked surprised.

"Well, before a man is hanged, he is usually given a hearty breakfast. If you are going to die, better to die on a full stomach than an empty one," Scott replied.

No sooner had he spoken than "the windows of the house were blown out, the ceiling came down and soot from the chimneys was scattered everywhere." Scott scraped the dust from his two boiled eggs and swallowed them. As the shelling intensified, he tried to persuade one of the residents in the house to flee with him.

"He would not leave, he said he would trust God and remain in the cellar of his house until the war was over. Poor man. His body must be in the cellar still. For the last time I looked back and saw the place there was not one stone left upon another. Only a little brick wall remained to show where my landlord's house had been."

During the evacuation, Scott saw thirteen men die in a single explosion. Scott helped carry the "mutilated, twisted and bleeding" corpses and laid them side by side near an outhouse. "The bodies were probably never buried because that part of a city was soon a ruin," he speculated. When he finally made it safely to Vlamertinghe he went directly to the schoolhouse which had been taken over as a dressing station. There, he observed, "a terrible shortage of stretchers and blankets" as most of the medical equipment had been lost at Ypres.

As soon as it was dark, the wounded began to come in, and by midnight the schoolhouse was filled to overflowing. The men were lying in rows on the cold stone floor with nothing under them. Ambulances were coming and going as hour after hour passed by. I went among the sufferers, many of whom I knew ... it was a strange scene. In the distance we heard the roar of the battle, and here in the dim candle-lit, hollow-sounding aisles were shadowy figures huddled up on chairs or lying on the floor. Once the silence was broken by a loud voice that shouted out with startling suddenness, 'O God, Stop it!'

When he returned from the field hospital to where he was staying in Vlamertinghe there was a letter waiting for him from his son Harry in Montreal, who was about to enlist and join his father. Harry had recently married Constance Hall, the daughter of a prominent Montreal family, but like his father, felt duty-bound to go to war.

> Well old man, from rumours I hear you seem to be venturing into dangerous places. Don't do anything rash, as those German shells are not to be trusted to choose between combatants and non-combatants. We have had a letter from William. He said he will have to wait about a month before he gets his glass eye.... He said he didn't feel he had done his bit and would like to get a commission out here on his return. I hear you are the best known man, officer or not in the First Canadian Division. That's pretty fine and naturally my bosom filled with pride to think that I had the discrimination to pick you for a father.

One evening as Scott walked from Vlamertinghe to Ouderdom he saw an old woman bent in prayer before a large black cross silhouetted against the crimson sunset. The crucifix in the roadside shrine stood long after the village was levelled. Later that night, unable to sleep because of a heavy German barrage, he thought of those who had died as he wrote "Requiescant."

It appeared in *The Times* on June 19, 1915.

In lonely watches, night by night
Great visions burst upon my sight
For down the stretches of the sky,
The hosts of dead go marching by.

Strange ghostly banners o'er them float,
Strange bugles sound an awful note,
And all their faces and their eyes
Are lit with starlight from the skies.

The anguish and the pain have passed
And peace hath come to them at last,
But in the stern looks linger still
The iron purpose and the will.

Dear Christ, who reign'st above the flood
Of human tears and human blood,
A weary road these men have trod,
O house them in the home of God.

Chapter Four

SCOTT REJOINED HIS BRIGADE in March, 1915, where he caught wind of rumours that during the Battle of Ypres Germans had crucified Sergeant Harry Band, a Canadian with the 48th Highlanders, leaving him to die hanging from a barn door with bayonets through his hands and feet. While many claimed the incident was true, everyone had a different version of what had happened. Other stories aimed at demonizing the enemy were being circulated, among them the tale that the Germans had made soap from the bodies of Belgian and French civilians and "children had been nailed like rats to the doors of houses." Suspicious of such rumours Scott inquired into the truth of the crucified soldier and concluded that, while there might have been some basis for it much of it was largely pure hearsay, "that someone told somebody, who told somebody else about it." He could find no reliable eye-witness accounts or any conclusive evidence. "We have no right to charge the Germans with the crime. They have done so many other things equally bad, that we need not invent charges against them unless they can be proven." Nevertheless, the story of "Canada's Golgotha" was used as Allied propaganda, and the Christ-like image of a soldier with bayonets through his hands and feet was, in the words of Robert Graves widely circulated to "make the English hate the Germans as they had never been hated before."

It was spring, and as he was driven to Robecq, 30 kilometres from Armentières. Scott, who claimed he never paid much attention to flowers,became more observant. "A wild flower growing in a ditch seemed to me to be almost a living thing, and spoke in its mute way of a life of peace and contentment, and mocked by its very humility the world of men now full of noise and death."

It was while he was at Robecq that Scott encountered Field Marshal General Douglas Haig who was getting ready for an unprecedented artillery barrage at nearby Festubert. Haig was a cavalry officer and a former member of the British Polo Team who rode everywhere on horseback with an escort of lancers. He came from the family of whiskey distillers but had a reputation of being puritanical, incapable of small talk, and in war historian Adam Hochschild's phrase, "was as stiff as the high collar of his dress uniform." His aide-de-camp, Desmond Morton, described him as a "silent man. You had to learn a sort of verbal shorthand made up of a series of grunts and gestures." Scott first "saw a man ride up carrying a flag on a lance. He was followed by several other mounted men. It was so like a pageant that I said to myself, 'Hello, here comes Joan of Arc.' Then the General appeared, and as he advanced we all saluted him."

Haig meant to win the war by "some Superior Power," which perhaps is why he acknowledged Scott. Seeing the canon's clerical collar he rode over to Scott and asked him if he had come over with the Canadians. ""I told him I had," Scott writes. "He replied, 'So glad you all have all come into *my* army." Scott didn't appreciate the condescension, "but thought it wise to say nice things to a General, so I told him we were all very glad too. He seemed gratified and rode off in all the pomp and circumstance of war."

The following day, riding across a bridge, he caught a glimpse of Arthur Currie, the first Canadian to be made a General during the war, and who, before the war was over, would be promoted to the highest rank in the British forces apart from Field Marshal. Currie was a general with the common touch who trusted his soldiers, and had "an almost fanatical hatred of unnecessary casualties." He had vaulted over senior officers to assume command of the Second Canadian Infantry Brigade. Known affectionately as "Old Guts and Garters," Currie proved to be a brilliant tactician who was devising the strategy for the capture of Vimy Ridge. In spite of orders to stay out of them, Scott spent the next couple of days in the dugouts around Le Touret preparing the soldiers for trench warfare. "I shook hands with them, but I thought it wise for a chaplain not to do anything which looked as if he were taking matters too seriously,: he recalled. "It was the duty of everyone to forget private feelings in the one absorbing desire to kill off the enemy."

Late one Sunday evening, as shells were falling in the fields, Scott held an outdoor service that ended with the hymn, "Abide with Me." The great red sunset glowed in the west and the trees overhead cast an artistic grey-green light upon the scene. The men were facing the sunset, looking towards Canada. As they sang "Hold thou the cross before my Closing Eyes," Scott was moved to write "A Grave in Flanders" in St. Jans Capelle, 1915":

> At night the tall trees overhead
> Are whispering in the stars;
> Their roots a wrapped about the dead
> And hide the hideous scars.
> The tide of war goes rolling by
> The legions sweep along
> And daily in the summer sky
> The birds will sing their song.
> No place this is for human tears
> The time for tears is done;
> Transfigured in these awful years
> The two worlds blend in one.
> The boy had visions while in life
> Of stars on distant skies,

So death came in the midst of strife
A sudden, glad surprise.
He found the sound for which he yearned,
Hopes that had mocked desire;
His heart is resting now, which burned
With such consuming fire.
So down the ringing road we pass
And leave him where he fell,
The guardian trees, the waving grass,
The birds will love him well.

When he arrived in Bethune, a railway and hospital centre, he was at last assigned a horse, not the "nag with knees ready at all time to sink in prayer," that he had been expecting. To his delight the horse he was given was a high spirited, part Arabian chestnut thoroughbred. Apparently the horse was meant for Sir James Willocks, commander of the Indian Expeditionary Force. But due to a mix-up in paperwork the horse was given to Scott instead. Scott named him Dandy.

"Dandy was a beauty and his lively disposition made him interesting to ride," Scott wrote "I was able now to do much more than parish visiting." Scott rode Dandy until war's end, until, after the armistice, the horse was shot to prevent it from being sold to the Belgian army. Major Francis Ware writes:

While Scott could never be classed as an expert rider, the Canon, for the next few years spent many hours in the saddle, and he used to tell of the happy times he and Dandy spent together, the ditches they cleared and the ones filled with slime and mud into which they fell, the signal wires that caught Dandy in the chest, or almost decapitated a distinguished padre, the fright which both often received when riding across a field to be almost blown to pieces as some hidden battery opened fire, but through it all, the darkness and the dangerous traffic packed roads, Dandy always brought him home safely.

Soon afterwards Scott acquired a white fox terrier which he named Philo which the troops jokingly dubbed his curate. The dog reputedly had a "great horror of shell fire," perhaps because it had been born in Beuvry, which had been heavily shelled during the war. Whenever Philo heard the roar of gunfire, he would "go into a state of whining terror, running round and round and barking furiously." Philo's fear of gunfire, however, didn't deter him from wandering into No Man's Land. Often, it would return covered with the blood of all the rats it had had found nesting in the corpses and had killed.

During his stay in Bethune, Scott often went to pray at the church of St. Vaast where he befriended the blind organist. He arranged for the organist to give a recital for the men in the chapel of the local monastery which the British had requisitioned as an ambulance headquarters. "There in the chapel, the blind man poured out his soul in the strains of a most beautiful instrument," Scott recalled. "We sat entranced in the evening light. He transported us into another world. We forgot the shells, the mud, the darkness, the wounded men, the lonely graves and the hideous fact of war. We wandered free and unanxious down the avenues of thought and emotion which were opened up before us by the genius of him whose eyes were shut to the world." The organist was killed when the church was destroyed by the Germans in 1918.

In July, 1915 Scott spent a week on leave in London where he had hoped to see Harry, who had just arrived in Bramshott, Hampshire, for training, but couldn't extend his leave to join him. "It is too bad you can't get leave just now as you certainly need a rest," Harry wrote to his father on July 9: "Don't have any compunctions about taking it whenever you can because you are entitled to it." Although disappointed that he was unable to connect with his father, he appeared to be in high spirits and eager to be moved to the front lines. He had "pretty reliable" information that he and his father could get together in France in August.

> You can expect me over there pretty soon. We are all working very hard all the time now, especially the field work. We spent the night in the trenches at Linchmere Common. Of course it had to rain torrents all night, so we had a rather uncomfortable time of it, but the men enjoyed the experience. About four o'clock I went to sleep in a dugout on a pile of sand bags (empty) and awoke in a few hours to find myself lying in a pool or lake of muddy water! We were inspected by the King, and H.M. expressed himself very satisfied with our appearance. Tom Firth sent me the ancient field glasses. They aren't half bad. I can see out of the other end quite distinctly. However I only carry them around and never expect to use them so the commanding officer can't jump on me for not having a pair. Well old man, come and pay me a visit as soon as you can.
>
> Your loving son, Harry.

Scott had no intention of having his leave extended. He felt "like a fish out of water" in London and wanted to return to the action as soon as he could. He bought small brass crosses to hand out to the soldiers all the while thinking "of the men in the trenches, their lonely vigils, their dangerous working parties, and the cold rain and mud in which their lives were passed." He also bought a tent which he could pitch anywhere so he could have a modicum of privacy. It gave him "great comfort and sense of independence." But, he wrote, comfort came at a price:

> When Philo and I retired for the night, we were really comfortable, but we were much annoyed by the earwigs and the inquisitiveness of the cows who could never quite satisfy themselves as to what we were. Many is the time we have awakened out of sleep in the morning by the sniffings and the sightings of a cow who poked around my tent until I thought she had the intention of swallowing us up. At such times I would turn Philo loose upon the intruder. Philo used to suffer at night from the cold, and would wake me up by insisting on burrowing his way down into my tightly-laced valise. There he would sleep until he got so hot that he woke me up again burrowing his way out. I hardly ever had a night's comfortable rest.

While he had been away the 1st, 2nd and 3rd Divisions had been combined into the Canadian Corps and placed under the command of General Alderson, with its headquarters at Steenje. Scott's friend, Francis Ware, was appointed Alderson's deputy assistant Adjutant-General. Scott's batman, Murdoch, was replaced with a private from the 16th Battalion by the name of James Ross.

The rules governing chaplains were changing too. Instead of being restricted in their movements, chaplains were being grudgingly accepted as parish priests within their battalions. The Senior Canadian Chaplain, Richard Steacy, who had been frustrated by interdenominational infighting, was sent back to Ottawa, and in the reorganization of the chaplaincy, Alderson offered Scott the job. Scott would report directly to the Chaplain-General's assistant, John Almond, a priest from Quebec City who had served in the Boer War. "The unexpected promotion opened up a life of almost dazzling splendour," Scott wrote. He moved to headquarters in the village of Nieppe, not far from Ypres, where he was given an office in a house owned by an old woman. "Round my bedroom window grew a grape vine, and at night, when the moon was shining I could sit on my window sill, listen to the sound of shells, watch the flare lights behind Armentières and eat the grapes which hung down in large clusters." He welcomed the promotion because he now had unrestricted access to the Front, where he could "be lost for a day and a night without being missed." He would, according to Ware, leave his batman Ross to do all the administrative work associated with his new position and cheerfully slip away to the Front singing Poo Bah's tune in *The Mikado*, "He never will be missed, he never will be missed."

Scott made the role of senior chaplain his own. He brought a new dimension to the job, and promoted what he described as "social Christianity," by expanding canteens, and the cinema and concert programs.

"The chaplain is not a soldier, and has no men, as a doctor has, under his command," he decreed. "His office, being a spiritual one, ought to be outside military rank. To both officers and men he holds a unique position enabling him to become the friend and companion of all." Scott also insisted that every man be given the religious privileges of their own denomination so that they could bear witness to the power of a universal God.

Young men are very seldom brought into contact with religion. In the war it was a revelation to them to find that there were principles and relationships of divine origin which allowed humans to overcome their difficulties ... there was a revelation to most men, in a broad way, of a mysterious soul life within, and of a huge responsibility to an infinite and an eternal being above. There was a revelation also, wide and deep, to many individual men, of the living force of Him who is both God and brother man. Where the association of church and home had been clean and helpful, men under the batterings of war felt consciously the power of religion. In the life at the Front there was much evil thinking, evil talking and evil doing, but there was underlying all this, the splendid manifestation in human nature of that image of God in which man is made. Men marched up through the mud and cold and darkness to face wounds and death, at such times, the sordid life has been transfigured before me. I have often sat on my horse on rainy nights near Hill 63 [a position 4 kilometres from Ypres held by the Germans] and watched the battalions going up to the line with wet rubber sheets hanging over their huge packs and with rifles on their shoulders, marching through the mud to face wounds and death. At such times the sordid life was transfigured before me. The hill was no longer Hill 63, but the hill of Calvary.

Scott often rode Dandy 35 kilometres a day from Nieppe to conduct funeral services at Ploegstreet and frequently held communion services in a private chapel at Kort Dreuve. In spite of having a horse to ride, it was still difficult to cover the ground between the services on Sunday.

One afternoon when I had been to the Cavalry Brigade at Petit Moncque Farm I had a great scramble to get back to the transport. In a bag hanging over the front of my saddle I had 500 hymn books. Having taken a wrong turn in the road I lost some time which was necessary to make up, and, in my efforts to make haste, the string on the bag broke and hymn books fluttered out and fell along the road. Dandy took alarm, misunderstanding the fluttering white things, and started to gallop. With two haversacks on my back it was difficult to hold on to the hymn books. The more the hymn books fluttered out, the more Dandy bolted, and the harder Dandy bolted the more the hymn books fluttered out. ....I reflected that it might really be a scattering of the seed by the wayside, and that some poor, lone soldier wandering from the paths of rectitude may pick up hymns by chance and be converted.

As Senior Chaplain he was required to co-ordinate services for each brigade, but his plans were often frustrated by the demands of senior officers. Generals would order an inspection at the same time that Scott had arranged a communion service, or the paymaster would arrive just as a service had been scheduled. "The paymaster, in the eyes of the men, took precedence over everything else," Scott observed. More often than not his arrangements for a service were frustrated "by a sudden order for the men to go bathing." Every time this happened, the adjutant would smile and tell Scott, "Cleanliness is next to Godliness." Scott held his tongue but thinking of the 39th Psalm would under his breath reply, "I held my tongue with bit and bridle while the ungodly was in my sight." General Currie replaced Alderson and moved his Corps Headquarters to St. Jans Cappel, which became "a great Canadian centre." The disadvantage was that it was a long way from the Front and Scott now had to ride 25 miles a day to conduct burial services for those who were slaughtered. trying to capture Hill 63. Because the road was hard on Dandy, Scott sometimes borrowed another more heavily-built horse. One slippery November day, that borrowed horse took a tumble and Scott was laid up for six weeks with a knee injury. While he was

Canon Scott on Dandy, the Arabian chestnut companion who "always brought him home," during the war.

recuperating he held a dinner for graduates of his old alma mater in Quebec, Bishop's College, who had enlisted. His first Christmas in France was not exactly cheerful. The roads were flooded, and on Christmas Eve, Scott was called to bury several soldiers who had been killed. Orders had been given not to exchange fire with the enemy on Christmas Day, and Germans climbed out of their trenches and left bottles of beer as presents to the soldiers they were fighting against. Scott celebrated Midnight Mass in a barn where three large biscuit tins covered with a Union Jack were used as the altar. It would have been, said Scott, "a fitting setting for the tableau of the Nativity." On Christmas Day, Scott wandered through No Man's Land to enjoy the sunshine and the soft, spring-like air. "There was nothing to disturb our Christmas peace and joy," Scott wrote. "Many Christmas parcels had arrived and the men were making merry with their friends." As he surveyed the battleground Scott was struck at how time had been suspended as both sides celebrated the birth of a child born in Bethlehem, and felt "that the angels had not sung in vain their wonderful hymn, 'Glory to God in the highest, and on earth peace towards men of good will.'"

The goodwill could not last. At the end of January Scott learned that Harold Heber Owen, of Vancouver, the twenty-two-year-old son of another Canadian chaplain, had been killed while leading a trench raid near Ieper. Harold's father, Cecil Caldbeck Owen, Chaplain of the 29th Battalion, was so distraught that Scott conducted the burial service, his voice "being at times almost drowned out by the rattle of machine guns and spitting rifles." Shortly before young Owen died he wrote to his mother that every friend he had made within the contingent had been killed. "It may sound unutterably selfish, but war is robbed of all its tinsel, glory and pomp when a hero friend smiles his last, while another hypnotized by the spirit of wholesale sacrifice steps into his place with no hope of ever coming back ... The

Canadian division put not only its hand but its body and soul into the breach and suffered it to remain, broken and mutilated. Those who survived ask themselves: 'What right have we to live when the rest have been taken?'"

By the spring of 1916 Scott's division had taken up quarters in Hooggraaf and in the neighbouring town of Poperinghe, the site of the military prison. Scott held a service for the prisoners and insisted that everything be done "as nicely as possible." Most of those in jail had been incarcerated for military offenses, and therefore, in Scott's view, were not common criminals. As he began a service, he asked the men to choose a hymn they wished to sing. A voice from one of the inmates shouted to a roar of laughter, "Here we suffer in grief and pain."

Scott often encouraged soldiers to speak their mind. On occasion the consequences of the open dialogue were more than he bargained for. During one of his question periods Scott said he would be pleased to answer any troubling question that any soldier wished to ask.

I want to ask a question which has been a load on my mind for a number of months now. Often I wake up in the dugout with my hair standing straight up and one eye looking into the eyeball of the other, trying to obtain an answer to this burning question. I have kept my weary vigil over the parapet at night, with my rifle in one hand and a couple of bombs in the other, and two or three grenades in each pocket, and still I ponder this burning question: When, Padre, do you think this fucking war will be over? Sir!

Chapter Five

In May, as Scott was on his way to Hoograven, the religious centre of the Netherlands, Dandy bolted and Scott was thrown. This time he broke his wrist. He wound up in the hospital housed in a Cistercian monastery high on the top of a high hill called Mont des Cats overlooking Flanders Field. To the north as far as the sea and to the east where the trenches were, he could see tracer shells bursting. While he was recuperating disaster followed disaster. First there was news of the Easter Uprising in Dublin which threatened to undermine the war effort, then there were reports of the inconclusive Battle of Jutland, in which the British and German navies fought to a draw. That was followed by the fierce attack on Mount Sorrel where Canadians were, in Scott's words, "reddening the soil with her best blood." Then Lord Kitchener, who was on a diplomatic mission to Russia was killed when his armoured cruiser, *HMS Hampshire,* hit a German mine and sank in gale force winds. Scott held a memorial service for Kitchener in the monastery chapel, then with his arm still in a sling, checked himself out because, as he declared, "a hospital is no place for me when Canadians are suffering."

He talked a colonel into giving him a side car ("If you don't give me a side car, I will recite one of my poems") and drove to Vlamertinghe to tend to the wounded. Among the dead was General Malcolm Mercer, the most senior Canadian officer to die in combat. "It was indeed an anxious time," Scott wrote. "Those ambulance journeys were things to be remembered ... The road was crowded with men, lorries, ambulances, transports and motorcycles. Every now and then the scene of desolation would be lit up by gun flashes. We had a hard time retaking lost ground. Gallant were the charges which were made in broad daylight in the face of heavy machine gun fire. Still, in spite of the reversals, the spirits of our men never declined. They were full of rebound and quickly recovered themselves."

While he had been in hospital his dog Philo wandered away or was stolen and, never one to be without a dog, he adopted a Brindle Bull terrier which he named Alberta. He was stationed at Corps headquarters at Abeele, where he settled into a predictable routine and participated "however humbly, in the making of human history." The daily routine was as follows:

> 8 a.m. Celebration of Holy Communion at St. George's Church
> 9:15 a.m. Parade Service for the Division.
> 11 a.m. Service for the Divisional rest camp
> 3 p.m. Service for the Grenade School
> 4 p.m. Service for the Divisional Train
> 6:30 p.m. Service for the 3rd Field Ambulance
> 8:45 p.m. Service for the convalescent camp

By June 1916, when another of Scott's sons, twenty-two-year-old Elton volunteered, preparations were underway for the third phase of the Battle of the Somme, or "The Big Push," as it was called. Field Marshal Douglas Haig launched the offensive on July 1, with a bombardment that echoed as far away as London. Sixty thousand men, including more than seven hundred with the First Newfoundland Regiment, were killed in a single day. For the next four months, wrote the correspondent Phillip Gibbs, "The tide of the wounded flowed back from the fields of the Somme in endless columns of ambulances. Row on row the badly wounded were laid on the grass outside the tents or on blood stained stretchers …" In spite of the unfathomable carnage, and mounting casualties, morale remained high. Haig recognized the role the chaplains were playing in rallying the troops. "We must, I think, give a good deal of credit for this to the parsons," Haig wrote to the King. "I have insisted on them preaching about the cause for which we are fighting … some parsons that were of no use were sent home. But taken as a whole, they have been a very great help to us commanders."

The character of war completely changed with tank warfare at the Somme. Tradition-minded British generals were brought face- to-face with modern warfare. Scott was no longer able to view war through the rosy glow of heroic sacrifice. "Modern warfare has taken all the romance and chivalry out of fighting," he griped. "The old feudal concept of war has passed away. The army will be looked upon in the future as a class of citizens given the necessary but unpleasant task of policing the world." He went to work at a little shack above the ruins at Contalmaison dispensing coffee and biscuits. "As we passed over the ground which had been won from the Germans, we were amazed at the wonderful dugouts which they had built and the huge craters made by the explosions of our mines. The dugouts were deep in the ground, lined with wood and lighted by electricity. Bits of handsome furniture, too, had found their way into them from the captured villages, which showed that the Germans must have lived in great comfort."

As the Somme offensive dragged on Scott described it as, "a time of iron resolve and hard work."

The price we are paying for victory is costly and one's heart aches for the poor men in their awful struggle. Ghastly were the stories which we heard from time to time. One man told me he counted three hundred bodies hanging from barbed wire which we had failed to cut in preparation for an attack. Another officer told me how his company had to hold on to a trench hour after hour under terrific bombardment. He was sitting in his dugout when a young lad came in, only eighteen years old, and his nerve utterly gone. He had come into the dugout, and like a child clung to the officer with his arms. There was nothing to do but to hold on and wait. Not long afterwards a shell struck the dugout and the boy was killed. When we retired, I had to leave his body there.

A piper [Jimmy Cleland Richardson, from Vancouver with the 72nd Seaforth Highlanders of Canada] won the Victoria Cross for his gallantry in marching up and down in front of the barbed wire playing his pipes while the men were struggling through it in their attack upon Regina trench. He was killed going back to hunt for his pipes which he had left behind while helping a man to safety. [The pipes were lost in the mud for 90 years, and when they were found were given to the B.C. Legislature where they are now on display.] This was war indeed, and one wonders how long it is to last?

On August 11, Scott's son Harry arrived in Hoograff with the 87th Battalion 4th Canadian Division, but missed seeing his father by a day. Canon Scott's division had been moved to new Chaplain Service Headquarters in St. Omer. In a hastily-pencilled note to friends he had left behind in England Harry wrote,

It is funny how absolutely different one feels now that one is right in it. I used to think I'd either be very scared or very excited, but at present I feel rather bored. I have no doubt, however, that a few hours in the trenches will change my feelings pretty quickly. We have eight days in the front line, eight days in the trenches, then eight days of peace in rest billets—that is provided everything goes smoothly and the Hun isn't too active.

The letter mentions an unnamed town near the Front "which received a present of 2,000 shells from the generous Hun, but things have been quiet since we arrived. However, we may expect a change at any moment."

Canon Scott spent most of August travelling through Picardy with the 3rd Field Company of Engineers. He returned to Amiens to visit the cathedral which he had last seen in 1883. "The sunlight was streaming through the glorious windows and the whole place was filled with a beauty that seemed not to be of earth," he recalled:

There was a large congregation present and it was made up of a varied lot of people. There were women in deep mourning, Sisters of Charity and young children. There were soldiers and old men. But they were all one in the spirit of humble adoration and intercession. The organ pealed out its noble strains and the whole place was vibrant with devotion.

Two years later the German Army levelled the cathedral.

In September Scott divided his time between a dressing station in a schoolhouse in Albert and another ward in the "Red Château" at Courcelett, where "torn and broken forms racked with suffering, cold and wet with rain and mud, hidden under muddy blankets, lay in rows upon the brick floor. Sometimes their heads were entirely covered, sometimes the eyes were bandaged, sometimes the pale faces, crowned with matted muddy hair, turned restlessly from side to side… then one by one, the stretchers would be carried to the tables in the dressing room." He witnessed an especially ghastly case —a French-Canadian soldier whose body from the waist down had been blown away by a shell that had exploded at his feet. "The case was hopeless, so he was covered up and carried out into the room reserved for the dying. Scott knelt and prayed until he died. As the body was removed, he took the man's pay book, and saw "that for some offence, he had been given a long period of field punishment, and that his pay had been cut to 70 cents a day. For 70 cents a day he had come as a voluntary soldier to fight, and for 70 cents a day he had died this horrible death. I felt like dipping that page of that man's pay book into his blood to blot out the memory of the past. The doctor who attended the case told me it was the worst sight he had ever seen." Conditions at the Red Château were especially gruesome. There were about three hundred men crowded into the Château, and "the air was not particularly fresh. Our choice lay between foul air within and enemy shells without. Naturally we preferred the foul air." Scott grew accustomed to eating his meals "in a place where rags saturated in human blood were on the floor in front of me. Two years before it would have been impossible."

Scott was relieved to move to Tara Hill in October where he and Harry were at last reunited for a week. Harry's battalion had set up camp on high ground in preparation for one of the final battles in the Somme offensive. From his window at Tara Hill, Scott could "see dear old Harry's tent," as he watched the officers and men of the 87th walking about. "He is a splendid fellow and the idol of his battalion." On October 17 Scott autographed copies of his latest collection of poems, *The Gates of Time*, which he planned to give to friends and family. He sent a copy to Willie, in which he wrote, "It is a lovely but misty morning. Harry went out to the trenches this morning at 5 a.m. God Bless and keep him safely. We are leaving this morning. They dropped some bombs on us last night." That was an understatement. The bombardment was so heavy the position had to be evacuated and Scott left Tara Hill for safer ground at Rollencourt, where he was lodged in a small "filthy little room" in a house on the St. Pol Road. He was unable to make himself comfortable in the room, and during a fitful sleep during a rainy night, thoughts of his brother's death in Wisconsin came back to haunt him. Inexplicably Scott was filled with a strange feeling of foreboding. The rain stopped. There was a knock on the door. He answered it to see a forlorn old man with an envelope in his hand. Without opening it, he knew Harry was dead.

Harry had been killed the morning of October 21, 1916 during the Battle of Ancre Heights and died in a filthy ditch, "a dreary, weird hollow" known as Regina Trench just as the Somme offensive was coming to an end. He was twenty-six-years old, and had married four months before leaving for Europe. He had been kneeling in a shell hole checking his watch when he was brought down by machine gun fire. The body was buried where it fell, because Scott did not want "living men to risk their lives to bring out the dead." Later that day one of his corporals, Jack Evans, marked the grave with a large and a small cross, 'suitably engraved.'

Scott informed his wife that their son "died with nobility, he didn't suffer. I hope to recover his body later. May God give you courage and strength. We must keep on unflinchingly to the end." Several weeks later he returned with a runner to No Man's Land to look for his son's grave. He had with him a map that indicated the approximate location of the shell hole where the body was supposed to be. But the ground had been plowed by shells and the trench was slippery with soft clinging mud in which, as the poet

Harry's first cross at Adanac Cemetery, Albert, France, circa 1926.
McCord Museum, MP-1982.64.122

The King commands me to assure you

of the true sympathy of His Majesty and

The Queen in your sorrow.

Secretary of State for War.

Condolences from King George V.
McCord Museum.

Edmund Bluden put it, "skulls appeared like mushrooms," Scott sank into the quagmire and found it difficult to manouvre. But he pressed on.

I was baffled in my search, and told the runner I was prepared to stay there for six months if necessary. I was not going to leave until I found Harry's grave.

We walked back along the communication trench and turned into one on the right, peering over the top every now and then to see if we could recognize anything corresponding to our marks on the map. Suddenly, the runner pointed far away to a lonely white cross that stood at the point where the ground sloped down through the mist towards the Regina trench. We made our way to where the white cross stood out in solitude. We passed many bodies which were still unburied. When we came to the cross, I read my son's name on it, but as the corporal who had placed the cross there had not been quite sure that was actually on the place of burial, I got the runner to dig the ground in front of it. He did, but we discovered nothing but a large piece of shell. Then I got him to try in another place, and still we could find nothing. I tried once again, and after he had dug a little while, he came upon something white. It was darling Harry's left hand, with his signet ring upon it. They had removed his identification, revolver and pocket book, but the signet ring (a stag's head engraved on a distinctive black stone) was on his hand. It was a miracle to think that I had found him on that waste on which I could see so many bodies still unburied—to think that I was able to touch his dear old hand once more, and know that he was there.

There are various accounts of what happened next, each of them invariably embellished. Major Ware, for one, insists that Scott, determined to read the burial service over his son's body, ignored the enemy gunfire. With clerical robes flowing in the breeze he made the sign of the cross. With that, according to Ware, the Germans stopped firing and allowed Scott to finish the service.

A million men died in four-and-half months of fighting. Scott could not fathom the idea that all of those who were slaughtered had died in vain and simply ceased to exist. Harry, and all those who died, "had been sanctified by death," he wrote, with the belief that "in the healing process of time all mortal agonies, thank God, will be finally obliterated." Acceptance and sacrifice were the building blocks of Scott's faith and he was not about to expunge them in favour of something more accommodating.

Harry's body was exhumed at the end of November and buried in the cemetery at Tara Hill. "I am so proud of my boys," he wrote. "Fancy being the father of two boys who have shed their blood for the Empire." Scott placed a crucifix in Harry's memory near the chancel arch in the 15th-century church of St-Riguier in Rollancourt. It is still there.

Chapter Six

VIMY RIDGE RISES 60 METRES and stretches for five kilometres above the gently rising Douai plains in Flanders. It had been captured and fortified by the Germans early in the war and it seemed impregnable. Bunkers deep enough to house an entire battalion had been built into it, and parallel trenches protected by barbed wire, pill boxes, dugouts and machine guns made it one of the strongest defensive positions in all of France. Previous attempts to capture the position had been ghastly failures. The French armies twice tried to take it, and the British attempt in 1915 failed. As one German taken prisoner of war boasted, "You might get to the top, but you will be able to take all the Canadians who get to the top back in a rowboat." By March, Scott, who had been ill with trench fever, was back in Ecoivres with his division. There he saw troops with the First Canadian Division involved in meticulous tactical planning as they studied a large model of Vimy Ridge in preparation for yet another attempt to take the position. Sir Julian "Bongo" Byng, who commanded the Canadian corps, delegated Major General Arthur Currie to plan the attack. Working with Andrew McNaughton, a young McGill University scientist and artillery expert, and three British physicists, new flash-spotting and sound-ranging technology was used to determine where precisely on the ridge the German guns were. New platoon tactics had been adopted, and soldiers were being taught how to move on a duplicate battleground in self-sufficient "blobs" behind a moving canopy of machine-gun fire above their heads. Troops had been trained for battle before, but never with such precision.

Scott was in a château at Ecoivres where a large model of Vimy Ridge had been built for all the officers and men preparing for the battle so they could be briefed on the character and contours of the land they were expected to cover. The Canadian attack on Vimy Ridge was scheduled for Easter Sunday, April 8, but it was postponed until the following morning. As 15,000 front line troops in 23 Canadian battalions were moved into position, Scott had no choice but to cancel Easter week services. He was 27 kilometres from Vimy Ridge when the attack began. Because of the timing of the attack Scott was confident that the engagement would mark a turning point in the war, and be the beginning of "a resurrection to a new and better life."

In the early morning hours of Easter Monday it began to snow. Scott climbed to the top of Bruay Hill overlooking the battlefield. There he knelt and offered a payer to "the God of Battles for the honour of our country." Precisely at zero hour, 5:30 a.m., "The whole countryside was lit up revealing the location of hundreds of unseen German batteries as thousands of guns—heavy, seige, howitzer and field—burst forth in a mighty thunder," wrote one eyewitness. From his vantage point, Scott could see "flashes of guns like lightning in all directions, and far over the German trenches, bursts of flame and smoke in a long continuous line, and above the smoke the white, red and green lights of surrender from the terrified enemy. Now and then our shells would hit a German ammunition dump, and for a moment, a dull red light behind the clouds of smoke added to the grandeur of the scene."

Within five hours the ridge was overrun and captured. It was a quick and stunning German defeat which marked the first Allied victory after two and a half years of war. British troops to the south reeled under a German assault and were driven back 20 kilometres beyond the Somme as the German storm troopers advanced and recaptured lost ground. The Canadians, however, further to the north around Vimy Ridge, held their ground in spite of a German gas attack. Scott was in the chalk pit near Vimy Ridge the following day, April 9 when the enemy launched the heaviest bombardment he had ever experienced. "There was a burst of artillery fire, and over our heads, with the usual swishing sound the gas cylinders sped forth. The German lines were lit with bursting shells. Up went their rockets calling to their artillery for retaliation. The display of fireworks was magnificent. A great artillery duel like that in the darkness of the night had a very weird effect and was wonderful to behold." Scott could hear "the gas bells ringing to warn the men of the poison that was being poured upon them." Soldiers weren't quite as enthusiastic. The next day Scott heard himself being ridiculed by soldiers who dismissed their padre as being more foolish than fearless. "There we were, out there with shells falling round us, and who should come up to us but the Canon, and the first thing the old bugger says to us is 'Boys, what a lovely night it is.'"

Even though 3,800 Canadians lost their lives, Scott insisted the victory was "a glorious moment. The attack which we had looked forward to and prepared for so long had been successful. The Germans had been taken by surprise and the important strategic point which guarded the rich coal fields of Northern France were once again in our possession." As he tramped over the battlefield, Scott was impressed by the trenches the Germans had built.

They had been strongly held and fortified with an immense maze of wire. But now they were ploughed and shattered by enormous shell holes. The wire was twisted and torn and the whole of the region looked as if a volcanic upheaval had broken open the crust of the earth. Hundreds of men were now walking in all directions. German prisoners were being hurried back in scores. Wounded men, stretcher bearers and men following up the advance were seen on all sides, and on the ground lay the bodies of friends and foes ... our burial parties were hard at work.'

In the greater scheme of war it was a minor victory for the British, but for Canadians Vimy became a defining moment in the young nation's progress. As the *New York Times* presciently noted, the capture of the ridge would be "in Canada's history, one of the great days, a day of glory to furnish inspiration to her sons for generations."

In the melancholy aftermath of victory Scott composed "The Silent Toast" to commemorate those who died in the assault, which is still read in many armouries in their annual salute to fallen comrades:

> They stand with reverent faces
>   And their merriment give o'er
> As they drink the toast to the unseen host
>   Who have fought and gone before.
>
> It is only a passing moment
>   In the midst of the feast and song,
> But it grips the breath as the wings of death
>   In a vision sweeps along.
>
> No more they see the banquet
>   And the brilliant lights around;
> But they charge again on the hideous plain
>   When the shell bursts rip the ground.
>
> Or they creep at night, like panthers,
>   Through the waters of No Man's Land,
> Their hearts afire with a wild desire
>   And death on every hand.

And out of the roar and tumult,
Or the black night loud with rain
Some face comes back on the fiery track
And looks in their eyes again.

And the love that is passing woman's
And the bonds that are forged by death,
Now grip the soul with a strange control
And speak what no man saith.

The vision dies off in the stillness,
Once more the tables shine,
But the eyes of all in the banquet hall
Are lit with a light divine.

Following the capture of Vimy Ridge a small church of thanksgiving was built out of corrugated metal for Scott at a place called Arriane Dump. It had a belfry and was topped with a phosphorescent cross that glowed in the dark. Inside there was an altar with a crucifix and candles, and the Union Jack as a frontal. The windows were covered with waxed linen, and it even had a portable organ. Tacked above the door was a sign: "St. George's Church."

The first service in the tiny church was a funeral for a soldier with the 2nd Division. By now, death had become so routine to Scott it no longer seemed to be a terrible thing, but something to be expected daily and dealt with uncomplainingly. As he put it: "In the midst of life we are in death, in the midst of death, we are alive." A communion service in the church was held daily at 8 a.m., and evensong every evening at 6 p.m. When Scott left Arriane Dump the makeshift church was turned over to the Senior Chaplain of the British Division, who had it moved 25 kilometres down the Arras Road to Roclincourt, and had a painted window of St. George slaying the dragon installed. Although Vimy Ridge had fallen, a number of surrounding villages remained in enemy hands. Scott packed bully beef, pork and beans, and biscuits into his haversack and followed the men as they liberated the towns of Arleux, Fresnoy and Willerval. In a dugout at Willerval he sat with officers who drank several bottles of wine while he thought about "the charming place it must have been in the days before the war." With Alberta at his side, he sat in a quiet place by a ruined brick wall and tried to disentangle the curious sensations which passed through his mind as he felt the breeze slightly fanning his face, smelled the scent of flowers, heard the skylarks singing, saw the broken houses, and listened to the shells which every now and then fell on the road to the east of the village. The warm spring sun beat down from a cloudless sky and "the glorious romance of being out in the war zone added to the charm. That super sensitiveness to the charms of nature thrilled me with delight."

He returned to the Somme where he placed a cross over Harry's grave then returned to the battlefield, where, to his dismay, he found mangled bodies of a number of Canadian and German soldiers, still unburied. Even though it was impossible to identify any of the dead, he said a prayer over each one. "The moan of the wind seemed like the great lament of nature for her sons who had gone," he wrote, "one could hardly imagine a scene so desolate and forlorn. The scene was too painful, and made too great a pull on the heartstrings, for among the slain beneath that waste of mud were many whom we had known and loved with that peculiar love which binds comrades in the fighting line."

The victory at Vimy Ridge heartened Scott. Shortly after he found himself living in a chalk cave known as the Labyrinth. "It had once been the scene of fierce fighting…deep down in passages scooped out of the chalk were the various offices of the division and the billets for the staff." The place was very crowded, and Scott quickly perceived that "the last person who was wanted there was a Senior Chaplain."

He continued to ride Dandy so he could conduct thanksgiving services for various battalions and brigades. On May 13 he celebrated Mass for three infantry Brigades who, standing together, "made a magnificent show of young, ardent and stalwart manhood." Scott lived for the camaraderie of his "parish visits" and the satisfaction that being with the men in the siege batteries gave him.

> I had meals with Generals in their comfortable quarters, sometimes with company officers, sometimes with the non-coms, but I think the most enjoyable were those that I took with the men in dirty cook-houses. With a dish cloth they would wipe off some old box for a chair, another for a table; then getting contributions of cutlery, they would cook me a special dinner and provide me with a mess tin of hot tea. When the meal was over and cigarettes had been lighted, general conversation was indulged in and there would be talks of home, of war experiences and many discussions of religion and politics. One question which was asked again and again was—'are we winning the war?'

In appreciation of his ministry the soldiers not only built a second St. George's Church for Scott, this time on the grounds of the Château d'Acq but a rectory as well fashioned out of tar paper. Charles Francis described the location as "pretty as any I have seen in France ... a long avenue of sycamore trees runs out to the main road and in the front is a park of beautiful trees not send out in any special order but dotted over a carpet of lovely green grass. Great spreading trees, sycamores, copper beeches etc. with most luscious foliage." The church architect, Colonel "Sandy" McPhail, a staunch Presbyterian who claimed that he was a descendant of St. Paul

(McPhail in Gaelic mans 'son of Paul'), was so pleased with his handiwork he instructed Scott to "baptize, marry, and ordain" men in the church. When Scott wondered aloud who on the battlefield would need to be baptized, married or ordained, the Presbyterian was earnest in his reply:

Like the centurion in the Bible, I am a man under authority. All I have to do is call up ten men and say 'go and be baptized and they will go. If they don't they will be put in the guard room. Then I will call up ten men and say 'Go and be married' and if they don't I will put them in the guard room. Then I will call up ten more and tell them, 'Go and be ordained in Scott's church'. If they don't I will put them in a guardroom.

In reality, a soldier was indeed baptized in the little chapel by a Roman Catholic chaplain while Scott was away on leave. He decided to take a break and visit Paris, Chamonix and Mont Blanc. Wartime Paris disillusioned him.

She wore the air of shabby gentility, the streets were not clean, the people were not well dressed, the fountains no longer played. France had been hard hit by the war, and the ruin and desolation of her eastern borders were reflected in the metropolis.

Most of his time in Paris was spent steering men away from brothels.

I can imagine nothing worse for a lonely young fellow who had taken his leave after weary months on the front line than to find himself in the midst of heartless gaiety… on all sides the minions of vice, diseased in mind and in body, lay in wait for their prey. It was a spectacle which filled the heart with anxiety.

Before he left Paris, he wrote to the *Continental Daily Mail* suggesting that some of the hotels be converted into hostels for enlisted men. He was back at Army Headquarters at the Château d'Acq by July 1, 1917, where he participated in the spirited celebrations marking the 50th anniversary of Confederation. From there he went on to Braquemont, a mining village just east of Dieppe, overlooking the English Channel. There he was housed in a company house where he enjoyed "linen sheets on the bed and an electric light at my side. It did not seem at all like war, but the end of the mahogany bed and some of the chairs and a corner of the ceiling has been perforated by bits of shrapnel. So even in the midst of luxury there was a constant reminder that the war was still going on—a death's head at the feast."

He had been made aware of plans for an imminent three-phase attack on a position called Hill 70, a little northwest of the coal mining city of Lens, and decided to walk from the Château d'Acq to the Front to witness the battle first-hand. Two British divisions had been annihilated on its slopes and now Canadian "Shock troops" were being sent in. As his batman, he was assigned a soldier who had been a heavyweight champion boxer. "People used to wonder why I had a prize fighter attached to me," he wrote "I told them that if the junior chaplains were insubordinate I wanted to be able to call in someone in an emergency to administer discipline. I always added, with perfect truth, that since my prize fighter was attached to me, I had no trouble with any of my chaplains." To relieve his anxiety, Scott often recited his poems aloud to anyone who might listen, something that the men he cornered into listening didn't always appreciate. As he was on his way to Lens he met an artillery officer, and they started walking just as artillery shells began to fly overhead. Scott began reciting one of his poems.

I was halfway through when the enemy began to shell the place and some bits of mud and brick fell in the road not far off. In spite of the beauty of my poem, I was faced with the problem of either hurrying the recitation (and thereby spoiling the effect of the rhythm), or of trusting his artistic temperament and going on as if nothing had happened. I did the latter, and continued reciting, unmoved by the exploding shells. I thought the Major would see that the climax of the poem had not yet been reached and was worth waiting for. I was mistaken. He became more and more restless, until at last he said, 'Excuse me Canon, but I think I must be hurrying on.' He left me on the road standing there with the last part of my poem and its magnificent climax still in my throat. He went back to his battery and told his friends there that I had buttonholed him and insisted that he listen to a miserable poem of mine, while shells were falling.

He arrived at Lens on the starlit morning of August 15, 1917, mere hours before the attack on Hill 70 was about to begin. Scott remembered the "great silence, stirred by only the morning breeze over the wide expanse of darkness." As the creeping Canadian barrage moved 90 metres forward, the Germans sent a rolling barrage of oil drums into the assault troops, drums "burning with pillars of liquid fire whose smoke rose high in the air with the peculiar turn at the top which looked like a giraffe." By sunrise Scott could make out, "silhouetted against the morning sky, men walking over the crest of the hill, and now and then jumping down into trenches they had captured. Once again, our Division had got its objective." But before the exhausted Canadians could consolidate the position, the Germans counterattacked with mustard gas. The toxin easily penetrated clothing and infected the skin. "There is nothing more horrible than to see men dying from gas. The body as well as the throat and lungs are burned and blistered," Scott wrote. There was nothing he could do to relieve the suffering. "So strongly were the clothes saturated with the poison that as they were being cut off, in order that the bodies of the men might be washed, our eyes and throats smarted from the fumes." He conducted the memorial services for those killed taking Hill 70. During one such service held in a wide green field, Scott was especially moved to learn of the death of Sergeant Frederick Hobson, an Englishman from Simcoe, Ontario. Hobson had dug a Lewis machine-gun which had been buried by shellfire out of the mud, rushed the enemy and opened fire until the gun jammed, then used it as a club to bludgeon and bayonet 15 enemy soldiers before he himself was cut down. (His Victoria Cross is on display at the Canadian War Museum in Ottawa.)

After the service, a bomb fell on the house in Bruay where he had been staying and he was forced to move to nearby Barlin where he found shelter above St. Joseph's Bar A number of men found it ironic to hear that their teetotalling padre was now living in a tavern. Scott reassured them that he was able to make himself right at home in any drinking establishment that was under the distinguished patronage of Canada's patron, St. Joseph. During a stopover in Cambligneul, he attended a "stag dance" in the local Y.M.C.A. The master of ceremonies was a soldier in drag called "Babs," and during the course of the evening "great burly chaps" danced with each other with "such gusto that the place was filled with sounds of dissipation." As the dancing continued "fast and furious," Scott, too, found himself on the dance floor, "amid roars of laughter." Scott found some of the jokes making the rounds in the charged homoerotic atmosphere rather vulgar and "mildly suggested" the men tone down their humour. After the dance, Scott broke up a street fight between two drunken soldiers. One of them grabbed Scott by the arm, and, in a stupor, insisted that the good padre enlighten him on the "theological differences between Anglicans and Presbyterians. I forgot which he was himself, but at the time the matter was of extraordinary interest to him," Scott wrote. "While I always considered it my duty to impart enlightenment to darkened souls, I promised to discuss the whole matter on our next meeting, and managed to tear myself away."

In October Scott was an unwilling witness to the draconian side of military justice. William Alexander, a platoon sergeant with the 10th Battalion had deserted hours before he was to lead his platoon in an attack on Hill 70 and was found guilty of cowardice. He had been sentenced to be shot at dawn. Alexander was a thirty-six-year old Englishman who had been orphaned at eleven and served with the King's Royal Rifles for eight years before he and his brother emigrated to Canada. He fought "exceptionally well" at Ypres. After being treated for a knee injury he was back with his men for the attack on Hill 70. But when he was needed no one could find him and a Corporal had to lead the troops into the battle. Two days after the fighting Alexander was found in a nearby village. He claimed he had been knocked unconcious by a shell before the assault even began. However, no evidence of any injuries were found when he was examined, and Alexander was arrested, charged with desertion, court martialled and found guilty. Canon Scott learned that there had been a history of mental illness in Alexander's family and, because of the tenuous evidence, frantically worked to have the death sentence commuted. He walked three kilometres to divisional headquarters through a driving rainstorm to plead with two generals for Alexander's life. There, he was told that the case was "utterly hopeless," and that only the Commander-in-Chief, Field Marshal Douglas Haig could reverse the sentence. Scott dashed back to the prison, arriving as dawn was breaking through the drizzling rain on October 18. He baptized Alexander and urged him to accept the inevitable with courage. While they were talking guards arrived and pulled a gas helmet over Alexander's head with the eye holes at the back so the condemned man could no longer see what was happening. He was then marched to the top of a nearby hill, seated on a box, and with his hands behind his back handcuffed to a post. A piece of white paper was pinned to his heart as a target for the firing squad. Alexander wanted the helmet removed but his last request was denied. Scott pronounced the benediction, and as he looked away, he heard the shots. "A young lad in the firing party absolutely broke down ... It was sickening," Scott wrote, "something quite unutterable." Scott presided over Alexander's burial at the Barlin Communal Cemetery. A cross on the grave makes no mention of how Alexander had died. "I have seen many ghastly sights in war, and hideous forms of death, but nothing has ever brought home to me so deeply and with such cutting force, the hideous nature of war and the iron hand of discipline, as did that lonely death on the misty hillside in the early morning," Scott wrote. He could not contain his revulsion, "While there are times that the prescribed penalty is justified, I am sure the British line, wherever it may be, will hold just as well without it," he wrote. An excerpt from his poem, "The Penalty," describes the execution.

> Would God that he had shared
> All that the others dared,
> And braved the thunderous fire
> Among the broken wire.
>
> But on his bandaged face
> No human sign can trace

The changes that are wrought
By agony of thought.

He sets his teeth and stands
With twitching, handcuffed hands,
His marked heart well in view,
God grant their aim be true.

A shuffling in the mire,
"Ready, Present—Fire"
He falls, and one man more
Has vanished from the war.

Alexander was one of twenty six Canadian soldiers who paid the supreme penalty for cowardice during the war. He was, of course, of what today wold be called Post-Traumatic Stress Distorder, a condition that was unheard of during the Great War. They were pardoned in 2001 and Alexander's name is today inscribed on page 603 of the Honour Roll in the Book of Remembrance in the Peace Tower on Parliament Hill. By war's end, there were nineteen military hospitals devoted to the treatment of patients who had been reduced by war to a state of gibbering helplessness.

Chapter Seven

Scott had been authorized to take only twelve men to Rome on furlough but the telegram giving him permission to do so was couched in such vague terms that he blithely ignored the directive and "knowing no one would take the trouble to look up the required file number," invited 46 soldiers, including two chaplains, to accompany him. Two of the men went AWOL in Paris but were picked up two days later and sent back. The rest of the entourage stopped at Monte Carlo, where they were prohibited from entering the casino because it was off limits to men in uniform, and continued on to Pisa to see the tower by moonlight before reaching their destination.

Rome ("Imperial city, slumbering on thy throne of vanished empire") invigorated him. He marched his party, two abreast, through the streets of the Eternal City to the Coliseum, took them to the theatre and placed a wreath on the equestrian statue of Victor Emmanuel. Scott had been to Rome twice before, in 1904 when he met Pope Pius X, and again in the spring of 1916, when he had a papal audience with Pope Benedict XV who had been elected Pope in 1914. Scott again arranged to have a papal audience for his men. "We had to wait quite a long time and at last the Pope entered clothed in white and looking much older and more worn than when I last saw him. He was very guarded in what he said to us, because we were the first soldiers he had received in a body, and any expression he might make with reference to the war would be liable to various interpretations," Scott wrote. "He spoke to some of the men in French and then wished us health and protection and a safe return to Canada."

While at the Vatican Scott also spent time with Cardinal Francis Aidan Gasquet, the English Benedictine monk and Vatican archivist who was an authority on the validity of Anglican ordination. From Rome Scott and his entourage took the train back to Florence, where they toured Santa Croce, a 13th-century Franciscan basilica which Scott described as "the Italian Westminster Abbey." As they were leaving the church they ran into a Marxist street parade, and were swept along into the boisterous procession. As Allies, Scott and some of the Canadians were carried on the shoulders of the demonstrators. The march had been organized by the left wing group *La società per porre fine alla Guerra* (the Society for Putting an End to War). Scott had little choice but to deliver an impromptu speech (in Italian) from the balcony of a local hotel. "I have wanted to be a member of your society for some time," he told the admiring crowd. After a dinner with local dignitaries Scott's party travelled back through Pisa, Turin and Paris before it returned in a drizzling rain to Poperinghe on the Western Front on November 5. It was the day before the last charge at Passchendaele. They could hear the guns, and saw "men coming and going in all directions."

The Allied offensive, officially known as the Third Battle of Ypres, had begun in heavy, never-ending October rains. The fighting, if you can call it that, turned the battlefield into mud, and continued through the heaviest torrential rains in 30 years. As British, Australian and Canadian troops inched closer to the little village of Passchendaele, No Man's Land was reduced to hundreds of thousands of shell holes with water six feet deep. "From the darkness on all sides came the groans and wails of wounded men," recorded Edwin Vaughn, a nineteen-year-old lieutenant, caught up in the action. "Faint long sobbing moans of agony and despairing shrieks. Dozens of men with serious wounds must have crawled for safety into new shell holes, and now the water was rising above them." Six weeks of fighting had resulted in 585,000 casualties, including 15,000 Canadians who managed to advance five miles of ground. The weather, not the enemy, ground the operation to a halt. As one lieutenant, Claude Williams, described it, "Talk about mud here. There is nothing but Mud, mud mud and more mud and nothing but more mud. You should see us coming out of the trenches plastered from helmet to heel with it, inches thick, even our hands and face."

As Scott wandered through the trenches near Goudberg Copse to survey what remained of the village of Passchendaele, he found "the whole region unspeakably horrible. Rain was falling, the dreary waste of shell-ploughed mud, yellow and clinging stretched off to the distance as far as the eye could see." The dead lay where they had fallen. Yet even in all the desolation, as he came across the body of a soldier who had had been killed that morning, Scott was moved by the terrible beauty of war. He described the horror of the scene with the detached observation not far short of outright admiration. The dead man, he wrote, "covered with a shiny coating of yellow mud looked like a statue made of bronze. He had a beautiful face, with finely shaped head covered with close curling hair and looked more like some work of art than a human being."

In the late afternoon, as the dead were being buried, shells fell near enough to splatter him with mud. He wandered about the desolate landscape and found a wounded soldier with a hideous wound on his back knee deep in water stained red with blood. "He was smiling and cheerfully made no complaint about what he had suffered." Scott located a stretcher bearer, and the wounded soldier was carried off the battlefield, " still happy to be alive, and apparently in good spirits."

Not so, Canada's Prime Minister. Robert Borden, a meticulous logician and moralist was so incensed at the appalling casualties that at a meeting in London shortly afterwards he grabbed the British

Prime Minister, Lloyd George,and shook him by his lapels. "Mr. Prime Minister, I want to tell you that if ever there is a repetition of the Battle of Passchendaele, not one Canadian soldier will leave the shores of Canada as long as the Canadian people entrust the government of their country to my hands." In a letter to Canada's High Commissioner in London Borden was scathingly critical of the way the British were running the war. Canada, he wrote, "can hardly be expected to put 400,000 or 500,000 men in the field and willingly accept the position of having no more voice and receiving no more consideration than if we were toy automats ... is this war being waged by the United Kingdom alone, or is it a war being waged by the whole Empire?" Borden had introduced the Military Voters Act, which gave all soldiers the right to vote, and he had gone to Europe, in part, to win their support for an election he was about to call on the conscription issue. When the war began, there had been roughly three Allied soldiers for every two Germans; now there were four Germans for every three. By the spring of 1917 Canadian casualties were outstripping enlistments by more than 2-1. British forces needed to find 600,000 men to replace their losses. If the war of attrition was to continue, and Canada was expected to contribute its share, men would have to be forced to go to war. Borden introduced the Military Service Bill which drafted men between the ages of twenty-three and twenty-five, and formed a coalition Unionist government with sympathetic liberals to get it passed.

Scott hitchhiked to Divisional Headquarters at the Château de la Haie, "a large house of no distinction." What did appeal to Scott about the château, though, were the "delightful grounds," and an outdoor theatre built into the slope of a hill that could accommodate a thousand. There he took to the stage to beat the drum for conscription. As Scott pointed out, "It was a critical time. Our manpower was being exhausted. Recruiting under the voluntary system had become inadequate to meet our needs. Beyond this, however, one felt that the moral effect of Canada refusing conscription would be very harmful," he reasoned. "The Germans would at once see Canada was growing weary of fighting and they would consequently take heart. It was most essential that our men should cast a vote for the coalition government."

After what they had endured, many soldiers on the front lines were often reluctant to expect others to join them against their will. Scott countered their hesitation to support the measure. "I told them I was in no way going to influence their vote. All I wanted them to do when they went to the polls was to make the sign of the cross in front of Borden's name." On December 17, 1917, Borden's Unionist government swept the country with 67 per cent of the vote and 153 seats, Laurier's Liberals took 82, but the conscription issue tore the country apart. Riots broke out in Quebec City and four civilians died.

Scott was back in Bruay for Christmas, "in the familiar neighbourhood with all the beloved Battalions around." The mining town had escaped shelling and he managed to hold "a beautiful but solemn" yuletide service on the stage of the local theatre as he had done before. During the New Year's Eve service, which was attended by more than 400 men, trumpets sounded the Last Post, and Scott asked that a ten-minute silence be observed before the recessional hymn, a deep-throated, stirring rendition of "O God our Help in Ages Past," was sung. Scott was moved by the extraordinary devotion.

There is something more subtle, more supernatural behind the life of men than one might gather from the King's regulations. The truth is, there is a revelation to most men, in a broad way, of an infinite and an eternal being above, a revelation wide and deep of the living force of Him as both God and brother man. In the life of a soldier there is much evil talking and sordid behaviour but underlying all of this, there is the splendid manifestation of that image of God in which man is made—self-sacrifice, living comradeship, and the unquestionable faith in the eternal rightness of right and duty.

As the New Year, 1918, was ushered in at midnight, Scott had "a wild and strange vision: He saw again "the weary waste of mud at Vimy, the fierce attacks at Arleux and Fresnoy, the grim assault on Hill 70 and the hellish agony of Passchendaele as the ceaseless chiselling of pain and death was engraved deep into the heart of Canada, the figures 1917."

Chapter Eight

BY NOW THE WAR HAD BECOME the deadliest catastrophe in Europe since the 14th century when the Black Plague killed a third of Europe's population. Several "Canadian-like" snowstorms during the winter added to the misery. Nearly everyone had bronchitis as the soldiers dug into the trenches around Vimy and prepared to hold the ridge they had captured. Scott visited the trenches to give pep talks to the men, sincere in his growing belief that the war would be over by the end of the year. In January forty soldiers were confirmed by the Bishop of Pencier at Divion, among them Vaughn Groves, a brigade runner who Scott remembered as a "rather delicate lad about nineteen years of age (Groves' attestation papers indicate he was, in fact, twenty-four) who never touched liquor and had just the type of character for great deeds in the war." Groves would be wounded several months later. Scott remembered Groves because, even though he was injured, he offered his own blood to another more seriously wounded soldier who required a transfusion. So much blood was taken from Groves, he fainted in the dressing station and was sent to England to recover. Scott continued his rounds of "parish visits" in the trenches along the supply lines.

> The dugouts were curious places, the entrance steps were steep and protected by blankets to keep out gas. At the bottom would be a long, timber-lined passage dark and smelly, out of which two or three little rooms would open. Men would be lying about on the floor sound asleep and it

would often be hard to make one's way among the prostrate bodies. The officer's mess would have a table in it and boxes for seats. On a shelf were generally old newspapers or magazines and a pack of cards. In the passage, making it even narrower, were a few shelves used as bunks. At the end of the passage would be the kitchen, supplied with a rude stove which sent its smoke up a narrow pipe. In the trenches, the cooks were always busy, and how they served up all the meals was a mystery to me. Water was brought in tins and therefore was not very abundant. I have occasionally, and against my will, seen the process of dish washing in the trenches. I could never make out from the appearance of the water whether the cook was washing plates or making soup, the liquid was so thick with grease. However, it was part of the war, and the men did their best under the most unpropitious circumstances.

Scott was present at an officers' banquet at Camblain l'Abbé on February 14 where he heard Prince Arthur, the Duke of Connaught, recite his poem, "The Silent Toast." Of 800 officers who had arrived three years earlier, only 124 remained on active duty. The rest had been killed or wounded. Canadian losses had been horrendous. In three years of fighting, more than 25,000 men had died, 103,000 had been wounded, and another 5,000 were missing and presumed dead. "It was strange to look back over three years and think that the war which we thought was going to be over in a matter of months had now been protracted and was still going on," he reflected.

On February 19, 1918 Scott was present for the dedication service as Sir Arthur Currie unveiled a severe, plain white concrete cross at Les Tilleuls that was the first Vimy Ridge monument. "Many generations of Canadians in future ages will visit this spot in tribute to the heroism of those, who leaving home and loved ones, voluntarily came and laid down their lives in order that our country might be free," he wrote. The cross could be seen for miles and dominated the landscape until 1936 when it was replaced in by the twin Adriatic marble pillars of Walter Allward's massive yet dignified memorial.

Following the dedication Scott went on furlough to London but his leave was not pleasant. The war, it seemed, had sapped British resolve and to escape the mood of defeatism he encountered in the British capital he cut short his stay to rejoin what he called his "beloved war family." He returned to a German-made dugout which had been captured near Lens, for as he put it, "If we have to be at war, the happiest place is at the Front." Upon his return he had been making small talk with four sentries at the entrance to his dugout and had he lingered a few more minutes he would have been killed. Moments after he left the sentries and descended into the chalk pit a Germans pineapple exploded and killed the three men he had just been chatting with. Scott stood guard over the bodies until a stretcher party arrived and took them away. Then he returned to the dugout. That is where he was on March 21 when German storm troopers launched their counter-attack against the British Third and Fifth Armies. "Over our heads, with the usual swishing sound, the gas cylinders sped forth. The German lines were lit with bursting shells," he wrote. "Up went their rockets calling to their artillery for retaliation." Scott could hear the gas bells ringing to warn the men of the poison that was being launched. "It must have been," he added "a drenching rain of death. I heard gruesome tales afterwards of desolate enemy trenches and batteries denuded of men. A great artillery duel like that in the darkness of night and over a waste of ground on which no human habitation could be seen had a very weird effect."

After three days of fighting, the Germans recaptured lost ground, and were making headway as they closed in on Amiens. They were about to overrun the trench line, and Scott was handed a rifle and given two hand grenades to protect himself. As a padre, he refused the weapons.

"How will you protect, yourself sir, if the enemy gets into the trenches," the Major asked him.

"I should recite my poems. They put my friends to sleep, and would probably have the same effect on my foes," Scott quipped.

In fact, Scott had a horror of being killed in a dugout, so he went above ground and surveyed what can only be described as a surreal scene. Pacing up and down before him was a corporal with a rifle slung over his shoulder, bayonet fixed, singing at the top of his lungs as pineapples exploded around him. "If only I could have made a moving picture and a gramophone record of his song as accompaniment. We could have made thousands of dollars by an exhibition of it in Canada."

March 29 was Good Friday but in the chaos, only a few showed up for services. Scott made his way from the front lines safely to Arras where the 3rd Infantry Brigade was quartered. On Easter Sunday, 1918, with a candle stuck on top of his steel helmet he celebrated Mass in the Ronville sewers under Arras. Nineteen kilometres of caves and quarries had been tunnelled under the city, and at one point during the war, they housed 24,000 soldiers. "The candle flames twinkled like stars in all directions in the murky atmosphere, and the singing of the men resounded through the cave," and drowned out the noise of the enemy shelling the town above them. "There was a strange charm about dear old Arras which is quite indescribable," Scott wrote. "In spite of its ruined buildings, there was the haunting beauty of a quiet medievalism about the city. The narrow streets, the pleasant gardens hidden behind the houses spoke of an age that had passed. To walk in the small hours of the morning on the silent and half-ruined streets and squares was a weird experience. Surely, if ghosts ever haunt the scenes of their earthly life, I must have had many unseen companions with me on such occasions."

Stray dogs were running loose, barking and foraging for food around the Château d'Acq when Scott returned from Arras with Alberta tagging along behind him. The beauty of the place had been destroyed since Scott had been there last, and the hillside "looked like a Canadian lumber camp." Because the dogs were diseased and often a nuisance, orders had gone out for them to be exterminated and a sergeant was assigned to round up the animals and shoot them. Scott gave little thought to the directive. His dog, Alberta, was so well known throughout the Division he couldn't imagine anyone mistaking the padre's pet for a stray. Scott slept in a bed banked high with sandbags around it for protection. He compared it to sleeping in a tomb. After one especially restless night he left to visit to the front lines and asked his batman to cart away the sandbags. When he returned, that evening Alberta was nowhere to be found. The sergeant on "dog duty" had seen the animal playing in front of Scott's hut, presumed it to be a stray and following orders, shot it on sight. Scott retrieved Alberta's body from the pit where it had been hastily discarded. He dug a proper grave for the animal beneath a sprawling tree. The death of his dog left him trembling and incoherent with rage. Three years of bottled-up emotion exploded. He had seen men torn to pieces and die in every conceivable way yet the death of his faithful Alberta unleashed the anguish he felt. He conducted a formal burial service for the dog, which was attended by most of the men at headquarters. Then he nailed a grave marker to the tree:

Here lies Alberta of Albert
Shot, April 24, 1918

The dog that by a cruel end
Now sleeps beneath this tree
Was just the little dog and friend
God wanted her to be.

He rode Dandy to Cauroy to mourn—curiously the same place
he had been when he received word of his son's death. Wherever he
tethered Dandy he had someone guard the horse and wouldn't allow
anyone other than the person guarding the horse to come anywhere
near the animal. From Cauroy he went to Château de Villers-Chatel, a
modern building with only the tower of the original château, built in
1414, still standing. The Château, which still stands today as a resort
hotel, was owned by two countesses, each of whom had her own
apartments, and who entertained troops in their drawing room. On
the lawn outside was a large and elaborate cement grotto with a statue
of the Virgin Mary, beneath a huge chestnut tree, "rich in leaves with
low boughs branching in all directions," furnishing a naturally green
arbour. At the end of the lawn was a path through the forest. The trees
had been trimmed so that the boughs overhead were interlaced like
the vaulted aisle of a cathedral. It was, said Scott, "one of the most
beautiful places imaginable for a church service." On Sundays Scott
set his flag-draped altar up under the chestnut tree and held services
for about a hundred. He also gave lectures on his trip to Rome to
"occupy and amuse the minds" of the men—talks which he said were
light-hearted but "impregnated with the poison of morality."

The countesses were moved by piety to keep candles blazing
in the grotto at night, invoking the protection of our Lady.
Our staff, guided not by faith, but by sight, were much
worried by the strong light which could easily be seen from
a German airplane. However no one could muster up the

courage to question the devotion of our hostesses, and as a matter of fact, we never had any bombing raids at Villers-Chatel. It was a question among the officers as to whether our immunity should be attributed to the power of prayer, or to extraordinary good luck.

With the war grinding to a halt, Scott managed to wangle a machine-gun motorbike sidecar from the Machine Gun Brigade to make his 'parish' rounds easier. Although the cars were in short supply, Scott was told to keep it and say nothing about it. "Whether it was sent to me from heaven with the assistance of General Currie, or whether it was sent to me by General Currie on the advice from heaven is a theological question which I had no time to go into during the war."

By June, he was back for a brief respite at Cauroy (where he had been when Harry was killed) before the division headquarters moved back to the Château at Villers-Chatel. Scott was among the estimated 40,000 people who turned out to welcome Prime Minister Robert Borden to Tinques for Dominion Day celebrations on July 1, which Scott described as "a tremendous manifestation of Canada's glory at the Front ... the vast crowd which fringed the vast expanse of ground was quite the most thrilling spectacle that Canadians had ever seen," among them, "a vast host of noble young gentlemen who saved the honour and the freedom of our young country." Borden had travelled to London for an Imperial War Conference, but spent as much time as possible visiting the troops and consoling wounded soldiers. Flight Commander Billy Bishop, who had shot down 53 enemy aircraft, flew over the crowd, and Scott was so impressed, he arranged with another pilot, Johnny Johnson, to take him up for a plane ride. He was given a choice of flying in a new machine with an old engine, or an old machine with a new engine. He opted for the old machine with the new engine. Wearing a leather helmet, goggles and a fur-lined vest, the experience overwhelmed him.

It was a curious sensation to look down and see absolutely nothing between me and the church of Izel-lès-Hameaux, crowned by its sharp pointed spire with no cork on it. It was a lovely afternoon and the most wonderful panorama spread below us. The great plain beneath us was marked off like a chess board in squares of various shades of yellow and green, dotted here and there with little villages surrounded by the billowy crests of trees. We saw straight white roads going off in all directions, and beyond, towards the east, low murky clouds behind the German lines.

As the plane flew over the war zone the pilot took a dive to fire several rounds of machine-gun fire at the enemy below. Scott heard a bang and saw a ball of thick black smoke behind the aircraft as six shots were fired at the plane. In the heart-pounding excitement, Scott recalled, "one phrase which I had often read in the newspapers kept ringing in my ears, 'struck the petrol tank, and the machine came down in flames.' And the last verse of "Nearer My God to Thee" ran through my head." The flight continued over the German lines, over Vimy Ridge, above the Château at Villers-Chatel, and circled above the 1st Canadian Divisional Headquarters, where Scott wrote on a piece of paper, "Canon Scott drops his blessing from the clouds." He threw it out and watched as it fluttered towards a wheat field. "So it didn't do them any more good than any of the other blessings I have dropped upon them," he laughed.

Scott's son Elton was in Boulogne recuperating from the effects of a poisonous gas attack, so after the Dominion Day celebrations Scott dropped in to see him, then took a side trip to the walled city of Montreuil where the British Army was headquartered. He had been told the city was off limits, but decided to go anyway. "I had been able to do so many things that were forbidden during the war that I thought it would be worth trying." As he drove up to the entrance gate, a sentry saluted and waved him through the ramparts. "It was a delightful old French town, full of historical interest. The narrow streets and quaint old buildings carried one back in through to the days of chivalry and battles waged by knights in shining armour."

Scott had hoped to hold a service at Etrum to commemorate the fourth anniversary of the start of the war, but his hymn books were confiscated and his plans frustrated. Instead, he spent the day wandering the deserted city of Amiens with some Canadian soldiers. The streets were deserted, the cathedral had been bombed, its "noble interior looked very dreary, the floor of the nave being covered with bits of broken stone and glass ... the empty city gave one a terrible sense of loneliness."

He was now quartered in Etrun, 60 kilometres away, in what had once been the country home of Archbishop Pierre-Florent-André du Bois de la Villerabel, Archbishop of Amiens. "The interior had once been quite fine, but was now absolutely filthy....The dirt on the floor was thick and a sofa and two red plush chairs were covered with dust. The bed in the corner did not look inviting and through the broken window innumerable swarms of bluebottle flies came from the rubbish heaps in the yard."

It was stifling hot and there was no water for washing. Scott wandered through the building, and peered into the archbishop's room, which "wore an air of soiled magnificence." He had no sooner moved in, when, to his astonishment, he awoke to discover himself surrounded by the entire Canadian corps, 100,000 men strong, which had been moved into the neighbourhood by stealth. They had arrived for a counter-offensive that would be later known as the Battle of Amiens.

Preparations had been conducted in secrecy, and the Canadian soldiers were warned with a note in their pay books to keep their mouths shut. Because "The moving of the corps had been so splendidly conducted, and the preparations so secret," Scott was certain that "success seemed assured." The new offensive began on August 8 and caught the Germans unprepared. More than 500 armoured tanks were successfully deployed, planes were used to drop ammunition to the advancing infantry.

The hissing rain of shells though the air on a twenty mile front made a continuous accompaniment to the savage roar of the thousands of guns along the line. Those guns sent their wild music round the globe. Up went the German rockets and coloured lights calling for help and ever and anon, a red glow in the sky told us we had blown up an ammunition dump. The noise was earth shaking and even more exhilarating than the barrage at Vimy. I was so carried away by my emotions that I could not help but shout, "Glory be to God for this barrage." The German reply came, but it was feeble and we knew we had taken them by surprise and the day was ours.

By the time it was over, Canadians moved eight miles into enemy territory, captured 190 guns, 1,000 machine guns, and took 9,000 prisoners of war. To his delight, as the result of pure luck, Scott captured three by himself. The three had been pretending to be dead at the bottom of a shell hole. Scott saw them lying there and wondered how they had died. As he looked into the hole, he was startled to see one of the bodies move. Scott shouted 'Kamarad', and to his intense amusement, "the three men lying on their backs put up their hands and said, 'Mercy, mercy.' It was most humorous to think that three human beings should appeal to me to spare their lives. I told them in my best German to get up and follow me, and I called out to the Sergeant, "I have three prisoners."

Scott had always joked about capturing prisoners. "Whenever our men were going into action I used to offer $25 to bring out a little German who I might capture all by myself. I used to tell them not to bring me a big one, as it might look boastful for a chaplain. Here were three, ready to hand, for which I had to pay nothing. We stumbled on a company of the 2nd Battalion, and I called out to them, 'Boys I got $75 worth of Huns in one shell hole.'" Scott handed his prisoners "who looked as if they expected to have their throats cut," over to the sergeant, but not before one of the Germans gave him buttons and shoulder straps from his uniform as a souvenir.

Although the fighting continued it was, as German General Erich Ludendorff recognized, the beginning of the end, "the black day of the German army." To Scott, however, it was "a magnificent moment in the war which filled the soul with strange and wild delight." As he wandered across the battlefield he found "hideously wounded" German soldiers begging for water. He gave as many as he could a drink, and ministered to the dying. "As they happened to be Roman Catholics, I took off the crucifix which I wore around my neck and gave it to them. They would put up their trembling hands and clasp it, and kiss it, while I recited the Lord's Prayer in German. One man who had a wound in the abdomen was most grateful and took my hand and kissed it. It should be strange to think that an hour before, had we met, we should have been deadly enemies."

Scott caught a touch of the flu and after the battle was again sidelined. He went to visit his son's grave, which had been in German hands for six months. To his satisfaction, he found the cemetery where Harry was buried still intact. "Shells had fallen in it, and some of the crosses had been broken, but the place had been wonderfully preserved." He was photographed at the gravesite by Australia's official war correspondent Charles Bean, as he surveyed the rows of little crosses, and behind them "the wasted land battered by war and burned by the hot August sun."

Scott's division had moved on to Arras, and that is where he was on September 2, 1918 when the Canadian 5th Battalion broke through the German defensive position between the French towns of Drocourt Quéant. The Drocourt-Quéant Line was a line of barbed wire entanglements which the Germans thought was impregnable. "This was real war," Scott declared. "We were advancing daily. On all sides I saw gruesome traces of the fighting. For a time it was really exciting because I did not know what I should do if the Germans came. I could not fight, nor could I run away, and to fold one's arms and be taken captive seemed to be idiotic. All the time I kept saying to myself, "I'm an old fool to be out here."

As the victorious troops prepared to continue their push across the Canal du Nord on to Cambrai, Scott was moved well away from the action to Averdoignt. There he managed to wangle a side-car and a driver from his old acquaintance, Sandy McPhail, who was in charge of the Motor Machine Gun Brigade. In appreciation, he sent McPhail a thank-you note:

> Dear Colonel McPhail
> If I had but a tail
> I would wag it this morning with joy
> At your having provided
> My car that's one sided
> With a good and intelligent boy.

May your blessings from heaven
Abound in this war
And be seven times seven
More than ever before.

He was driven to Le Carouy, Arras, and then to Achicourt, where on September 22, in a small Protestant church, he celebrated what would be his last communion service in France. Instead of an altar, there was a high pulpit, and when he stood up in it, he felt uncomfortably like a "jack in the box." As he mounted the pulpit, he was filled with a strange sense of foreboding. "The thought of the near presence of the Angel of Death was coming to the mind," he wrote. He had always expected to be killed during the war, and began to wonder why he had survived when so many others had died. "At home in the cities of Canada, profiteers were heaping up their piles of gold, politicians were carrying on the government, or working in opposition, in the interests of their parties, while here in the mud and rain, weary and drenched to the skin, Canadians were waiting to go through the valley of the shadow of death."

It rained as the combat engineers prepared to cross the canal. Scott spent time with some draftees who were about to go into the front lines for the first time. He received permission to go on patrol with the newcomers provided he took off his white clerical collar and promised not to crack any jokes that might make the men laugh and give away their position. "To do outpost duty was more interesting than pleasant," he wrote, "for at all times, the sentries had to keep straining their eyes in the darkness to see if an enemy patrol was coming to surprise us." On one of the sorties the Germans dropped a gas shell, and a whiff of the poison burned his throat. Scott was "filled with alarm lest I lose my voice and be unable to recite my poems. It was hard enough to keep my friends long enough to hear my verses, but if I had to spell them out in sign language, no one would ever have the patience to wait until the end." His throat healed, and to relieve the mounting anxiety he read "The Unamed Lake" to a captive audience of officers of the First Battalion huddled in a dugout near Inchy, and rambled through the nine verses.

The recitation seemed to be so well received, he read another, several more in fact, until he noticed a curious thing. "No one stirred. I paused in the middle of a poem and looked around to see what was the matter, and there to my astonishment, I found that everyone, except the young Intelligence Officer, was sound asleep. I secretly consoled myself with the reflection that the one officer who was unable to sleep was the one who specialized in intelligence." The following day he had lunch with Major Roderick Bell-Irving of the 16th Battalion and dinner with General Herbert Thacker, the Commander of the First Canadian Division, who had been through the Boer War and had been the Canadian military attaché in Japan during the Boxer Rebellion. After dinner, Scott took Dandy for a ride. His horse was as "fresh and lively as ever," as they galloped through the fields. The sun was setting and Scott compared the fresh evening air to "a draught of champagne."

When he returned and turned the horse over to Ross he said, "I fear I may lose my leg, and I wanted to have my last ride." At five o'clock the following morning, with a barrage of fire, four infantry Battalions began the push across the canal. By the end of the day they had taken it. But the Germans were determined to check the advance. During their assault on Sunday, September 29, 1918, the feast of St. Michael the Archangel, Scott was helping a soldier who had lost a hand, to a first aid post near Battalion Headquarters. As they were walking an engineer came up to Scott and handed him a pair of binoculars. Scott stopped to adjust the focus on the spires of Cambrai, when he was caught in a burst of enemy machine gun fire.

"Earth was blown into our faces, we both fell down, and my eyes were full of dirt," he recalled. When he tried to get up, he realized the bullets had sliced the artery in the calf of his right foot. He "fell with a feeling of exasperation that I had been knocked out of the war."

Scott was taken to the dressing station at Haynecourt, where to relieve the pain, he drank his first shot of rum. From there he was moved to a Trappist monastery at Mont des Cats to recover. As the ambulance drove through the desolate countryside, twilight fell and night descended, Scott recognized that "the great adventure of my life among the most glorious men that the world has ever produced was over." While at Mont des Cats he learned that Major Bell-Irving, whom he first met aboard the *Andania* when they sailed for Europe, had been killed in a hail of German machine-gun fire at Cambrai. Scott was transferred to Endsleigh Palace Hospital in London where the nightmares began. "The hideous sights and sounds of war, the heart rending sorrows, the burden of agony, the pale dead faces and blood stained bodies lying on muddy wastes, all these came before me as I lay awake counting the slow hours and listening to the hoarse tooting of the lorries rattling through the dark streets of London," he wrote.

He was in the hospital on the eleventh hour of the eleventh day of the eleventh month, when the bells pealed to mark the end of the war. There was relief, but no real rejoicing. His poem, "Cease Fire," commemorates the Armistice:

> Over the broken dead,
> Over the trenches and wire,
> Bugles of God rang out—
> Cease Fire!
> Woe to those nations of men
> Who, in their heat or desire,

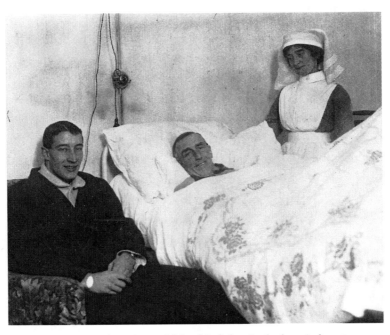

Lieutenant Elton Scott visiting his father in the hospital, 1918.
McCord Museum, MP-1982.64.71

Break that stern order of God—
"Cease Fire."

From his hospital bed he wrote to Amy that his thoughts were with the Canadians who would not return. "For four years they had been my beloved companions and my constant care. I had been led by the example of their noble courage and the unhesitating performance of the most arduous tasks in the face of danger and death, to a grander conception of mankind and a longing to follow them, if God would give me grace to do so, in their path of utter self-sacrifice. I had been with them in their joys and sorrows and it did not seem possible that I could go now and desert them in their bitter fight."

Scott was decorated with the Distinguished Service Order (DSO).

In spite of his eccentricities, he was regarded as a hero by the fighting forces, for as infantryman Harold Innis wrote, "The chaplain who does his turn in line with the men, who goes through the battle with them, has won a large place in the hearts of his men. The men loved him for in the hours of their misery, help and comfort radiated from his undaunted soul."

Scott returned to Quebec City aboard the *Empress of Britain* on May 4, 1919. He was now respected throughout the country as the dean of the 440 Canadian chaplains who had served during the war.

As he debarked he was moved when he was asked to inspect the Guard of Honour. "Each man was an original, for four years and seven months they had been away from home, fighting for liberty and civilization," he observed, "Many of them wore decorations; many had been wounded. No General returning victorious from a war could have had a finer reception."

He saluted the veterans and celebrated the First Canadian Expeditionary Force with "The Unbroken Line."

> We who have trod the borderlands of death
> > Where courage high walks hand and hand with fear
> Shall we not harken what the spirits saith,
> > "All ye were brothers there, be brothers here?"
>
> We who have struggled through the baffling night
> > Where men were men, and every man divine,
> While round us brave hearts perished for the right
> > By chaliced shell-holes stained with life's rich wine
>
> Let us not lose the exalted love which came
> > From comradeship with danger and the joy
> Of strong souls kindled into living flame
> > By one supreme desire, one high employ.

Let us draw closer in these narrower years
    Before we still the eternal visions spread;
We, who outmastered death and all its fears,
    Are one great army still—living and dead.

Chapter Nine

BEFORE THE WAR SCOTT was politically a Conservative who celebrated Sir Robert Borden's 1911 election victory over Sir Wilfrid Laurier, and then supported Borden's Unionist government during the war.

He returned a Fabian socialist.

While he continued to express his religion in poetic terms he returned more convinced than ever that the church had a moral obligation to redefine its role in society and contribute to the public good. As Duff Crerar writes in *Padres in No Man's Land*, "The war had been a crusade that offered Canadians a providential opportunity to realize a higher level of national righteousness." Scott had, of course, been a social activist in his own parish, but the Great War had transformed the homeland. The country had been profoundly broken— financially, morally and spiritually. Conscription had opened fissures and fault lines in the nation: farmers and workers began to organize as inflation hit everyone, pitting rural residents against city dwellers, labour against management, French against English. Returning soldiers, who had no benefits whatsoever, could not find work. The war had not only shortened lives but it touched families in ways that were both maddening and tragic. Among Scott's papers is a poem that imparts the spirit of human forgiveness the once stern moralist now found necessary to preach.

> Bill White came back and found his wife
> And in her arms a baby

At first he said it isn't mine
And then he said, it may be
So they lived for many years
A credit to their station
And all because he gave to things
A kind interpretation.

While counselling some returning veterans Scott heard of dis-
content and mounting civil unrest in Winnipeg It began as a relatively
small-scale conflict between the city's building-trade and metal-shop
workers. But set against the backdrop of massive unemployment, inflation, and the fear of Bolsheviks taking over the country, it exploded
into a general strike. To protest against the refusal by employers to
negotiate with unionized workers, 30,000 supporters, including returning soldiers who could not find work, walked off their jobs on May 15,
1919 and took to the streets in protest. Scott believed that collective
bargaining was a constitutional right and hopped the next train to
Winnipeg. He went, he said, as a mediator to express solidarity with
his brothers.

"All ye be brothers there, now be brothers here," he exhorted, a
theme that he repeated in "The Unbroken Line":

Let us not lose the exalted love which came
    From comradeship with danger and the joy
Of strong souls kindled into living flame
    By one supreme desire, one high employ.

Let us draw closer in these narrow years,
    Before us still the eternal visions spread;
We, who outmastered death and all its fears,
    Are one great army still—living and dead.

When he arrived in Winnipeg he declared his support for the strikers. "I am getting old, but I am going to dedicate the rest of my life to fighting labour's battles," he announced: "I shall go back to the east and tell them all my sympathies are with the strikers."

His remarks enraged Brigadier General H.J. B. Ketchen, Military Commander of the Winnipeg district. Ketchen was prepared to have Scott arrested for inciting the workers and charged with sedition. Instead, he declared him absent without leave from his Quebec City garrison post. Under the escort of two military policemen Scott was put on a train back to Quebec City. The next day, known as Bloody Saturday, ten strike leaders were charged with sedition, police confronted the strikers, and two men were killed and 30 injured. Scott was never disciplined. He had become a hero to the veterans, a spiritual leader who had put his life on the line, been wounded in action and now went to bat for them. Just as he had risked his life in war, he was prepared to risk his reputation to improve their welfare. In October 1919, he was at La Malbaie, a vacation retreat for Quebec's English speaking elite, where he conducted one of the first formal memorial services for the war dead in Canada. On the sixth anniversary of the capture of Vimy Ridge, Scott was at Rideau Hall where he was entertained by Lord Byng, Canada's Governor General. More than 150 officers who had served with Byng were invited to a state dinner with the Governor General and with General Currie. "It was wonderful to see how the bonds of comradeship forged by service at the Front causes us to gather in little intimate circles, gunner officers at one table, some engineers at another, the Third Brigade at another and the Red Patch division also gathered around one large table," observed Ware. "To make the evening complete, Canon Scott was also present and wherever he went he was the centre of a group happy to clasp his hand again."

Canon Scott conducted one of the first formal memorial services for the
war dead in Canada, La Malbaie, Quebec, October, 1919.
McCord Museum, MP-1982.64.52.

The Canadian newsmagazine *Saturday Night* named him one
of six outstanding Canadians. The profile of Scott stated that "when
the story of the war time activities of the Canadian army in France
has faded into cut and dried history, Padre Scott will still loom
up as a picturesque, romantic and a lovable figure." There would
be clerical honours as well. Lennox Williams was elected Bishop
of Quebec, and Scott was made an archdeacon in 1925. In typical
fashion, he accepted the title with a self-deprecating, buoyant sense
of humour.

> There was an archdeacon who lived in Quebec
> Who his body in apron and gaiters did deck
> And all the good women who saw the divine
> Exclaimed that his legs were remarkably fine.
> So finding at last where his beauty spot lay
> The vain archdeacon I am sorry to say

To show off his gaiters and hear what was said
Would stop in his sermon and stand on his head.

In 1926 an anthology of Scott's war poems, *In Sun and Shade* was published. He dedicated the book to his son Harry who had been killed. "Even as he trod that day to God, so walked he from birth, in simpleness and gentleness, in honour and clean mirth." Scott's youngest son, Frank (F.R), who had been away in England on a Rhodes scholarship had just returned to Canada when 12,000 coal miners in Cape Breton went on strike. The British Empire Steel Company, which had acquired the Dominion Coal Company, set out to break the coal miners' union. Scott and his son Elton joined the picket lines in support of the workers. He was, F.R. wrote, "angered by the miserable conditions of living, the utter lack of feeling amongst the directors and so forth." Scott's guiding principle had become "Be ye angry and sin not," from the Book of Ephesians (4:26-27), a verse which suggests that every Christian has a right to be indignant about wrong-doing and injustice. He befriended J.S. Woodsworth, the Manitoba circuit preacher who was elected to the House of Commons as a Labour Party member in 1921, and he began agitating for a Canadian-made socialist party that would be concerned with "supplying human needs, and not the making of profit." As the coal miners' strike dragged on, the company cut off the workers' line of credit at the company grocery store, relief funds were exhausted, and striking miners and their families faced starvation. In an open letter to Prime Minister Mackenzie King, published in the *Ottawa Citizen*, Scott warned that unless the government took action, Canada faced the prospect of a Bolshevik revolution.

"There is no law in the constitution of Canada which gives you the right to avert the hideous calamity now very imminent, the Supreme law of common humanity empowers you to intervene," he wrote:

The responsibility of the fate of our fellow Canadians rests not upon one province only, but on the whole Dominion. The ancestor whose name you so proudly bear was once judged a rebel because he stood for the rights of the oppressed in defiance of the law. An oppressed people is crying for a deliverer today. Never in the course of our history has there been a more wonderful example of patient heroism than is being manifested by the thousands of men, women and children in Cape Breton. If the agony of human beings does not move your government to immediate action, perhaps the reflection of that failure to save the lives of Canadians now will not only shake your government, but what is worse, it will shake the ordered constitution of our country. It is merely playing into the hands of Bolshevism, which we all dread, and which is threatening the governments of the world today. This should be the motive to lead us to play fairly with our fellow Canadians, but it not ought to have weight with those whose selfish interests shut their ears to the cry of the suffering....

In reply, King told the House of Commons that while he was not less anxious than Scott to see the existing distress speedily alleviated, without an appeal for assistance from the Province of Nova Scotia, he could do nothing. As language commissioner Graham Fraser suggests, both Scotts, father and son, felt that the Catholic tradition, with its greater emphasis on social obligations, would somehow mitigate the prevailing Protestant ethic of free enterprise. In 1932 F.R., with his father's encouragement, wrote *Social Planning for Canada*, and helped frame the Regina Manifesto which gave birth to the Co-operative Commonwealth Federation (C.C.F.). F.R. became a pacifist, and bluntly informed his father that if he was to have a

Mr. and Mrs. Scott at their son Harry's grave in Adanac Cemetery, France,
1923.
McCord Museum, MP-1982.64.124.

military funeral, he could not, in all good conscience attend. "That's perfectly all right, my boy," was Scott's reply. "I can assure you that I will be there."

When Sir Arthur Currie died in 1933, Scott delivered the eulogy at the memorial service: "He knew no fear of public opinion, and cared not for advertisement or praise. He was always himself, a Canadian first and foremost." Although Currie had been knighted, Scott said, "He never aped the manners or imbibed the class prejudices of those who, in the early days, might have looked down on the citizen soldier who had come from across the sea and took a front place among the military leaders who trained at Woolwich and Sandhurst."

During the first week of August, 1934, Scott attended the high-spirited reunion in Toronto marking the 20th anniversary of the beginning of the war. There he shared the podium with Viscount Allenby and Admiral Reginald Tyrwitt. An estimated 250,000 veterans assembled for the three-day reunion. He delivered a sermon in Riverdale Park attended by a quarter of a million veterans and civilians, who joined in the responses, prayers and singing of the 39th verse of Chapter 10 of St. Luke, 'He that loseth his life for my sake.' Scott reminded the crowd that he had used the same text twenty years earlier when he spoke at Valcartier the night before the First Expeditionary Force left for Europe.

It was in September and in front of the stage on which the chaplains stood were gathered 15,000 men from all over Canada. Mass bands rendered the music and the numbers of hymns were signaled from the platform. All around us, clothed in autumn glory, were the granite mountains of the Laurentian range. It was a cloudless day, and the peace of nature flooded the world with beauty. But at the back of our minds, a grim spectre, waxing ever more and more, filled us with an anxiety we never knew till then. It was the grim spectre of a war which even then in those days threatened the very foundations of our civilization. The concourse was indeed a notable one. All sorts and conditions of men were welded together in a compact and mighty mass by the fire of patriotism and the determination to endure unto the end. Men from every walk of life had rushed to the defence of the principles of our common heritage. Barriers of caste and exclusion were broken, and the thrill of a common resolve linked all hearts to One. Keep the bond sacred. Guard it at all times. Use the power that lies in it for the cause of the weak, the downtrodden and in the lives that still bear the scars of war.

It was in the middle of the Great Depression. Scott used the occasion to preach a social gospel as well. He was, he said, shocked by "the wild orgy of capitalist covetousness" that had led to unemployment, poverty and even starvation. He warned that "the very foundations of orderly government have been imperiled," and took note of the "mutterings again of war" in Europe where Adolf Hitler had just become Führer and Reich Chancellor of Germany.

"Where," he wondered aloud, "is the world we fought to establish?"

He quoted Alfred Lloyd Tennyson's "Ulysses."

> Tho' much is taken, much abides; and tho'
> We are not now that strength which in old days
> Moved earth and heaven, that which we are, we are;
> One equal temper of heroic hearts,
> Made weak by time and fate, but strong in will
> To strive, to seek, to find, and not to yield.

Later that evening he was carried aloft through the Royal York Hotel, as veterans sang, "What has become of Hinky-dinky parlez-vous? Haven't you told your wife of the girls you knew? You must have told your wife, no doubt. But I bet you left most of it out …"

As they caroused and snake danced through the lobby, a voice shouted, "Did you write that one too, Canon Scott.?"

As the evening progressed, revellers fuelled by alcohol barged noisily through the hotel and stomped through the corridors; a few began smashing the piano and other pieces of furniture in the lobby. Scott climbed on a polished table and by simply raising his hands was able to restrain them and restore order. "He had a wonderful way with the men, when he raised his hand his desire for quiet was always respected," Ware, who was there, tells us. "Woe to any man who disturbed the peace when the canon was talking. The men in no more than uncertain manner saw to it that the canon alone had the floor." Scott suggested everyone take a break to sing a hymn. Some suggested his favourite "Abide with Me," others wanted "Fight the Good Fight," but when someone called, "Onward Christian Soldiers," Scott surveyed the damage and chuckled, "No, none of us are being very Christian tonight."

Scott retired in 1935 and moved into a suite in the Château St-Louis which overlooked the prison on the Plains of Abraham. To his dismay, the view offered a clear view of executions which were conducted in the prison courtyard.

In 1936, Scott, Amy and their sons travelled to Vimy for the dedication of the National War Memorial. Like many of those who had survived the War to End All Wars, he could not bring himself to imagine that another war could be played out on the same battlefields of Europe. But if another war was to be fought, the old man was prepared

The Scotts on the occasion of their Golden Wedding Anniversary,
Montreal, Quebec, 1937.
McCord Museum, MP-1982.64.160.

to volunteer and do his part. In a letter to Major Ware who was now stationed in Regina, Scott said he was as eager as ever to return to active duty but added, "they would not take me overseas." Instead, he went on a speaking tour to urge those veterans who were still fit and able to do so to enlist and again fight for peace. "There is much to do, and so few who have the ambition to do it. There is still plenty of room for the spirit and courage which drove the Canadian corps to the top ranks among the world's fighting forces," he told audiences.

He turned eighty on April 7, 1941. Congratulations to the old warrior, who was still in good health, poured in from across the country. Editorial writers saluted him with affection as a priest who taught soldiers "when to play and when to pray." Newspapers honoured him on their editorial pages, as someone "greatly beloved in the army; who is still remembered with affection by veterans of the Great War, in the present war, his verse—and it is fine verse—seems to have received a new stimulus, a renewal of strength and beauty." In the darkest days of the Second World War, in a sign of absolute confidence of victory Scott walked to the Plains of Abraham where he chiselled a cross and the word CREDO into a rock. The stone, which he later painted white, is still located on the Plains to the east of the old prison.

Amy, "the queen star" of his life, died in 1943. Scott took comfort in the knowledge that they would not be separated for long. As he stood by her grave in Mount Royal Cemetery he felt himself surrounded by the circles of the dead, of all those soldiers he knew and had buried. There were no apparitions, no voices, but an absolute certainty that all had surrendered their lives to a loving God. In one of his last poems, he anticipated the end. "The long night falls, and we must forward to the battle lines, from this long raid there is no turning back, though we may stumble upon the broken track, some star will guide us with heavenly light, and as of old, we do not fear to die ..."

In August 1943, Prime Minister Mackenzie King invited Scott to the Château Frontenac where he read his poem, "The Charter of the Atlantic," to British Prime Minister Winston Churchill and U.S. President Franklin Roosevelt, who were in Quebec City to plan the strategic initiative that would result in the invasion of Europe.

Oh Tides and winds of freedom, bear the message o'er the sea
That evil shall not triumph, and men shall be free.
Two nations stand together as champions of the right,
Two beacons blaze together against the clouds of night.
Beware ye hearts of Satan, who blast each crippled land,
For God's avenger cometh, and the sword is in his hand.
His face is as the lightning, his anger swift and sure,

His name is truth and justice and his victories endure.
Beneath the mighty banner we face the bitter odds
We shall not faint nor falter for the cause we guard is God
We scorn the power of tyranny, and the challenge they hurled
And march with souls undaunted to liberate the world.

Four months later, in December, Scott suffered a serious bout of
pneumonia. His lungs were so congested that on Christmas Eve he
had to be hospitalized. By January 14, 1944 he appeared well enough
to be sent home. He had once said he wanted to have "an idle time
before I come to die … to listen to the wind and if I can, recall the
stirring things it said to me …"

He wasn't afraid of death. To Scott it was as much of a miracle
as being born. As he had written in "My Friend Death" :

Will death come to me robed in black
    With hollow eyes and toothless grin?
Will he have wings upon his back
    And hold the scales to weigh my sin?
Shall I behold his face with dread
    And strive to hide me from his sight,
When death sits down beside my bed
    On my last night?

I picture death quite otherwise
    Than such a spectre full of gloom,
As herald of the morning skies
    To chase the darkness from my room,
An emanation from that star
    Which lingers last above the dawn,
And sees the golden lands afar
    And night withdrawn.

I like to think his voice is low
  And filled with murmers of the sea,
Where tides forever ebb and flow
  And taste the joys of destiny,
If death be such, when'er he come,
  I shall lie tranquil to the end,
Then say, with lips to others dumb,
  "I go, my friend."

On January 19, 1944, as Canon Scott slipped in and out of con-
sciousness, his son, F.R. was at his bedside. Scott recognized him,
took his hand and murmured, "Is this the revolution?" They
were his last words. His full military funeral was conducted at St.
Matthew's by Philip Carrington, Lord Bishop of Quebec. At Scott's
request, there were no eulogies. Those would come ten months
later at the national memorial service sponsored by the Royal
Society of Canada held for him at St. Paul's Cathedral in London,
Ontario. Those present agreed with Bishop Renison's assessment
that Scott had been "the idol of the soldier, a legend from St. Julien
to Amiens. His escapades, his stories, his sermons in action, his
gaiety in the dugout made him a legend to the troops."

Scott had half-jokingly expected to be cremated and wished
to have his ashes buried beneath the floor boards at St. Matthew's.
He had even composed his epitaph: "*In this spot, in a pot, lies Fred
Scott.*" That was not to be. The casket, draped in the silk Union
Jack which he had carried with him through the battlefields of
Europe, was flanked by soldiers of the 8th Royal Rifles. Behind
the casket, Major Edward Fisher carried Scott's decorations and
service medals which had been laid out on a velvet cushion. As the
band of the Royal 22nd Regiment played Handel's "Dead March
from Saul," the cortège began the solemn procession through the
snow, down rue St-Jean to the train station. From there the coffin

was taken to Montreal where the body lay in state at Christ Church Cathedral, where "everyone in the crowd were the men who had known him in the mud in Flanders." Then it was taken up to the mountain by non-commissioned officers from the Royal Montreal Regiment where Frederick George Scott was buried beside Amy. When St. Matthew's Church closed in 1979 it was converted into a municipal library, but on its walls remains a tablet:

To the Glory of God
And in Loving memory
Of
1861 Frederick George Scott 1944
Priest and Poet, who for nearly half a century
Ministered as Priest of this Parish
And also served as chaplain with the Canadian
Expeditionary Force 1914-1918
Thine Eyes Shall See Him and be Satisfied

The Canadian War Museum acquired Canon Scott's ten service medals and other decorations in 2011 at auction in London for $28,000. They include his Companion of the Order of St. Michael and St. George, his Distinguished Service Order and the rare Royal Canadian Humane Association's gold Sanford Medal, one of the few awarded for gallantry in saving a life.

Epilogue

ANNIVERSARIES, LIKE MUSEUMS, provide an opportunity to reconsider the past and to focus attention on people like Scott who made history and to bring a new understanding to them in the context of their times. Scott's own memoir, *The Great War as I Saw It*, published in 1922, is the starting point for this appreciation. It is a rambling, restrained book written to celebrate the "great and glorious deeds" of our soldiers, so that "The ears of Canada may never grow deaf to the plea of widows and orphans and our crippled men for care and support." I have quoted extensively from the book, and have been able to annotate and elaborate on many of the harrowing experiences he wrote about.

Today, Frederick Scott would perhaps be dismissed as a somewhat arch, religious dinosaur. He was, however a gallant, civilized man, a self-deprecating dutiful priest, a dependable solider (who was not quite a soldier) and a poet with an evangelical concern for humanity. Nothing about him was morally ambiguous. He was not an especially warm individual but one who was admired for his self-assurance. He displayed a quick sense of humour in surprising circumstances. He was also a very lucky man. He survived. "He loomed larger than life, he was a bit imperious but his commitment to public life made him an important voice in the Canada that was emerging at that time," says Geoffrey Kelley, his great-great nephew. Scott was a conservative with a radical streak. Some suggest that Scott suffered from a martyr complex. But he did not go to war to get himself killed. When he enlisted he had no idea the war would last as long as it did or that he would lose a son in the carnage. He went, because as a priest, he believed in the quaint idea that he had an obligation to exercise the corporal acts of mercy—to visit the sick, to quench thirst, to bury the dead and to ransom those held captive. He ministered to all, and consoled allied and enemy soldiers alike. On the battlefield, denominational differences were irrelevant to him. He often confessed that he had a horror of being bombed in a dugout. But he accepted death and dying as a routine part of living, as a submission to God's will. Scott's convictions were shaped early on by a romantic appreciation of death. Infant mortality and life expectancy were lower in the Victorian Age. By the time Scott was twenty-four he had been orphaned, the first love of his life had died, then he lost a brother and a young son. Scott embraced a belief in the continuity of the spirit, in order, and in self-discipline. He was unflinching in the face of sorrow. His assurance that "God would provide" helped him survive the terror of war. While he was depressed by the death of his son, in Scott's mind those who were killed on the battlefield were martyrs to a noble cause, and like valiant knights on a sacred crusade, their sacrifice was not to be mourned, but celebrated.

The war, of course, changed everything. It made him sensitive to disability, injustice, poverty and grief, and it made him angry. He denounced the "monstrous futility of war as a test of national greatness" and he raged against "profiteers at home who were heaping up their piles of gold, and against politicians who worked in the interest of their parties, while soldiers, in mud, rain, weary and drenched, slogged through the Valley of the Shadow Death in order that Canada might live."

A spiritual leader, he was a hero to the veterans, and he delivered for them. Just as he risked his life in the war, he risked his reputation to work for a new social order after the war. During the Depression his resolve was channelled into a crusade for social justice.

Uncompromising in his own beliefs, he respected the convictions of others. What he left behind was the energy of his idealism.

Canon Scott never minded telling stories at his own expense. Once, while chatting with a Roman Catholic chaplain about their mission, Scott suggested that in spite of their denominational differences, both men were working for the same great cause, "I am doing it my way, and you are doing it your way ..."

"No," the curé interrupted him. "We both are doing it HIS way."

Selected Bibliography

Cook, Tim. *At the Sharp End: Canadians Fighting the Great War, 1914-1916.* Toronto: Viking Canada, 2007.

Cook, Tim. *Shock Troops: Canadians Fighting the Great War, 1917-1918.* Toronto: Viking Canada, 2008.

Crerar, Duff. *Padres in No Man's Land: Canadian Chaplains and The Great War.* Montreal and Kingston: McGill-Queen's, 1995.

Djwa, Sandra. *The Politics of the Imgaination: A Life of F.R. Scott.* Toronto: McClelland & Stewart, 1987.

Gillmor, Don. *Canada: A People's History,* Volume II. Toronto: Canadian Broadcasting Corporation, 2001.

Gwyn, Sandra. *Tapestry of War: A Private View of Canadians in the Great War.* Toronto: Harper Collins, 1992

Hanson, Peter. *Muddling Through: The Organisation of the British Army Chaplaincy in World War One.* Solihull. UK: Helion, 2013.

Hochschild, Adam. *To End All Wars: A Story of Loyalty and Rebellion, 1914-1918.* Boston: Houghton, Mifflin Harcourt, 2011.

Putkowski, Julian, and Dunning, Mark. *Murderous Tommies.* Pen and Sword: South Yorkshire, UK, 2012.

Scott, Frederick George. *A Hymn of Empire.* Toronto: William Briggs, 1906.

___. *Collected Poems.* Vancouver: Clarke & Stewart, 1934.

___. *A Hymn of Empire and Other Poems.* Toronto: William Briggs, 1906.

___. *In Sun and Shade: A Book of Verse.* Quebec: Dussault and Proulx, 1926.

_____. *In the Battle of Silences: Poems Written at the Front.* Toronto: Musson, 1917.

_____. *My Lattice and Other Poems.* Toronto: William Briggs, 1894.

_____. *Poems.* London: Constable & Company, 1910.

_____. *Poems Old and New.* Toronto: William Briggs, 1899.

_____. *The Gates of Time and Other Poems.* London: Samuel Bagster & Sons, 1915.

_____. *The Great War as I Saw It.* Toronto: F.D. Goodchild, 1922.

_____. *The Soul's Quest and Other Poems.* London: K. Paul, 1888.

_____. *The Unamed Lake and Other Poems.* Toronto: William Briggs, 1897.

Ware, Francis Bethel. *Canon Scott as I Knew Him.* Unpublished manuscript, McCord Archives. Box 13 of the Scott Fonds.